9.95

LEE COUNTY LIBRARY
SANFORD, N. C.

STAGE RIGHT

The author and his wife in one of their favourite presentations, as King Henry and Queen Eleanor in 'The Lion in Winter'.

STAGE RIGHT

*How to run
an amateur theatre group*

BRIAN MATTHEW

ADAM & CHARLES BLACK
LONDON

LEE COUNTY LIBRARY
SANFORD, N. C.

First published 1975
A. & C. Black Ltd
4, 5, & 6 Soho Square
London W1V 6AD

ISBN 0 7136 1575 3

© 1975 Brian Matthew

All rights reserved. No part of this publication may be reproduced, stored in a retrieval system, or transmitted in any form or by any means, electronic, mechanical, photocopying, recording or otherwise, without the prior permission of A. & C. Black Ltd.

*Printed in Great Britain by
Hazell Watson & Viney Ltd,
Aylesbury, Bucks*

Contents

		Page
Foreword		vii
1	Forming a Society	1
2	The Producer	8
3	The Stage-Manager	16
4	The Actor	24
5	Lighting	35
6	Costumes and Scenery	44
7	Make-up	60
8	Getting it all Together	71
9	Sound Effects	78
10	Voice Production and Diction	84
11	Movement on Stage	92
12	Advice to the Players	101
13	Front of House Management	114
14	Final Thoughts	120

Plates

Frontispiece
The author and his wife in 'The Lion in Winter'

Between pages 56 and 57

1. Realistic set for 'Rattle of a Simple Man'
2. Realistic set for 'Journey's End'
3. Open-air rehearsal of 'The Young Elizabeth'
4. Open-air performance of 'The Young Elizabeth'
5. Costumes with painted texture for 'Alice in Wonderland'
6. Mountains made from sheets for 'The Snow Queen'
7. One of the *mountains* opened to show the scene painted on the inside
8. Hand-stencilled wallpaper for 'The Heiress'
9. Use of small props on a small stage
10. David Jason and Brian Matthew in 'Dock Brief'
11. The dramatic effect of actors *not* facing each other
12. Grouping of players to focus attention on one of them
13. A pantomime horse

Foreword

Once upon a time there was a daily radio magazine programme called *After Seven*. Each edition had a different compere who was encouraged to stamp it with his own personality and to introduce items in which he had a particular interest. I was fortunate enough to be one of the team and my producer, Angela Bond, knowing my interest in theatre suggested a weekly item directed specifically at amateurs. I wrote about a dozen short talks, introducing advice stemming directly from personal experiences, and was pleasantly surprised at the enthusiastic audience response.

Even more surprising was a letter from a publisher saying that he had heard he talks and thought they would expand to book length with advantage. It agreed with him and hope that we were both right.

My thanks for the photographic illustrations are due to Harold Hammond, who took all the studies in our own theatre, and to Neil McHarry, an accomplished amateur actor and producer himself, for those taken at performances elsewhere.

The line drawings were provided by Wendy Bradfield who has designed and made many costumes and sets for my productions and now works in the same capacity in the professional theatre.

I should also like to thank everyone who has ever acted with me, either as professional or amateur, from RADA, through one-night stand fit-ups and weekly rep, to the Old Vic. What small knowledge and skill I may have acquired over the years is truly the outcome of their patience, kindness, guidance and unstinting assistance. Their names would fill a book far longer than this one.

Finally, my inexpressible gratitude to one man who has been with me in the amateur theatre ever since I began, over fifteen years ago. David Hart has lit every production I have ever done, which must be close on a hundred, and also controlled the lighting at nearly all the performances, of which I have lost count. He has often achieved miraculous results with inadequate resources, and has designed and built a lighting console of such staggering versatility that my imaginative powers are never likely to extend it to the full.

To all these people, and to those of you who read the book, may I, in emulation of the first actor I ever saw – the late Sir Donald Wolfit – grasp the edge of the curtain and say,

'from the depth of my being – I thank you.'

Brian Matthew
June, 1975

*To Angela Bond
for her enthusiastic encouragement at the beginning*

Chapter 1

Forming a Society

Professional actor friends have frequently asked me over the years why I bother to work with amateurs and I have always given the same answer. I believe that one can only develop and improve as an actor or as a producer by constant practice. In any year, during which those friends will usually have spent more time out of work than in, I shall have played at least half-a-dozen roles and directed as many plays. My performances will have involved as much personal effort as they would had they taken place at the National Theatre, and although the lack of facilities in a village hall is admittedly a handicap to a producer, the very deficiencies can be a spur to imagination.

Having said that practice is the best teacher, I should also emphasise that informed advice and guidance are invaluable. The self-taught enthusiast in almost any branch of art is likely to acquire certain bad habits which, as the years go by, become increasingly difficult to eradicate. A brilliant saxophone-player recently told me that he began by teaching himself and after a few months wondered why certain passages were almost impossible to play. He then took lessons, and discovered that he had been using entirely the wrong system of fingering. Similarly, an actor who has had no training will perhaps develop ungainly physical mannerisms and tricks of speech which make his work much harder than it need be, while the producer who doesn't follow certain precepts of direction may wonder why his imaginative ideas never seem to come to fruition.

I have tried to condense in this book some of the things I have learned over the years about the presentation of plays and offer it, not to the experienced amateur who probably knows more about the business than I do, but to newcomers in schools, for example, or in small village communities, who want to start a dramatic society. Reading it will not make you an accomplished actor or producer overnight, but it may help you to avoid some of the headaches and heartaches along the way and thereby lead to greater enjoyment for you and for your audiences.

Although presenting plays is very much a group activity which depends for its success on the total involvement and enthusiasm of all concerned, I have found by experience that the best results are always achieved when there is a leader, or figurehead, responsible for making major policy decisions. If you think for a moment about any celebrated professional company, you will realise that the brightest periods of its history have always evolved around such a personality. Committees are necessary for the efficient, businesslike running of a dramatic society, but let them not become involved in such matters as choosing plays and certainly not in casting. This can only result in hours of wasted time and often in fruitless argument.

So, let's consider first of all the basic requirements for starting a dramatic society. The most important appointment at this stage is unquestionably that of producer and although it is desirable to find someone with previous experience, this may not always be possible. You will, therefore, need a volunteer who is prepared to work twice as hard and long as everyone else for, as we shall see later, the producer starts before anyone else and is responsible for choosing plays, casting, preparing his own work, and supervising lighting, stage-management, sound effects, music and set design. He is at once a creative artist, an administrator, teacher, guide and friend to his cast, and he'd better be handy with screwdriver and paint-brush as well! Once such a paragon has been found, his decisions should be given wholehearted support even if you don't always agree with them. A dramatic society, like a ship, can only have one captain. Like a captain, the producer may delegate responsibilities to his officers while retaining supreme command.

The next most essential member of the team to the producer is the stage-manager and I often think that his is the most thankless task in the theatre. He's the one that everybody blames when things go wrong, but who seldom gets thanked when they go right. He's the producer's right-hand man in rehearsal, his deputy on occasions and his representative during performance. Very often he is required to combine his duties with playing a small part, but I should recommend that this is avoided wherever possible.

I have always been lucky, in the fifteen years or so that I have been involved with amateur productions, in having a magnificent lighting technician. An electronics engineer, he has designed and built a superb lighting console which is my pride and joy and the envy of all who see it, but he also has a deep dedication to all we attempt to do, sensitivity, and a strong dramatic sense. He must be something of an exception in the amateur theatre, but it nevertheless would seem to me of paramount importance that you find a lighting man who is at least a knowledgeable electrician, even if he knows nothing about theatre. We shall discuss later on some aspects of the technique of lighting, but I shall assume an acquaintance with the technicalities.

If it is at all possible, I should strongly advise adding to that team a designer for both sets and costumes. Many groups I have seen perform tend to muddle through these aspects of their work, with everyone lending a hand in a rather haphazard way. A producer should always have a good idea of what he wants his set to look like, but he will get much closer to it if he has someone who can translate those ideas into practical drawings.

So, with a producer, stage-manager, lighting technician and set designer, you have a team who can, between them, organise and mount a production. In subsequent chapters I shall deal at length with the work of each of them in turn, but I must emphasise that there are no very precise demarcation lines. They should all have a working knowledge of each other's responsibilities.

In passing, even if it is stating the obvious, let me say that in addition to your production team, you will find it essential to have a secretary and a treasurer. Every production entails a surprising amount of paperwork, and even if you work on a shoestring budget – and most of us do – there are still numerous expenses that need to be properly accounted for.

Now let's think for a moment about the choice of place in which your plays are to be presented. Not so long ago, a dramatic performance was almost unthinkable unless it could take place on a raised stage with wings and front curtain, in a hall with serried ranks of audience chairs. The amateur theatre in general follows the fashions of the professional theatre, and for years we were tied to the concept of the proscenium arch. Happily, there has been a revolution in this respect, with the development of thrust stages, theatre-in-the-round and so on. Plays are now often performed in pubs, restaurants, small rooms without stages and in every conceivable type of surroundings. In recent years I have acted in village halls, gardens, private houses, school gymnasia, churches, hospital wards and modern civic theatres. All you really need is space for an audience to sit, and space for the actors to perform, and that leaves the choice wide open. Actors sometimes complain about being required to perform in unconventional surroundings, but they can usually be convinced that doing a play anywhere is better than not doing one at all. There used to be a story, allegedly true, of a famous actor-manager auditioning a young aspirant who complained that he could not concentrate because of the noise of traffic outside. The actor-manager rose haughtily in the stalls and said, 'Young man, if you really want to be an actor, you should be able to perform in a public lavatory!'

What I hope I have emphasised is that, with a little ingenuity and imagination, a play can be performed almost anywhere. From a practical point of view I would merely make the proviso that it is desirable for either the audience or the acting area to be raised, even if this entails the construction of small, firm rostra. There are few plays which don't require members of the cast at some stage to sit, kneel, or even lie down; and no matter how brilliant the acting at such times, it will be utterly wasted unless the audience can see it.

When forming a dramatic society, a matter which will have to be faced at the outset is the cost of the operation. No matter how simple your production it cannot, alas, be put on for nothing. It would be pointless for me to attempt to quote actual figures here, because with the speed that prices are rising, by the time this gets into print those figures would be of little value other than historic interest. However, the areas in which you will have to spend money remain fairly constant, so let's see what they are.

First and foremost, of course, you will need a set of books for the play in hand. These can often be obtained from libraries, or from such organisations as the British Drama League and the National Operatic and Dramatic Association at a hire-charge which is a fraction of the purchase cost. However, I do advise that wherever possible you should buy your own books because, as will be explained later on, it is really essential for all concerned to mark these copies in a variety of ways. One word of caution: when calculating the number of copies you will need for any play, remember that in addition to the cast you will need one each for the producer, stage-manager, lighting technician, sound effects man and prompter.

Then we come to printing costs. The very least you will need is tickets for your audience, and I think that a programme of some sort is equally essential. This need not be elaborate, and it is often sufficient to roneo a typed sheet, but even this will cost something. Many societies feel the need to display posters about their forthcoming productions and to advertise in the local press, and this is something you can only assess against your own situation. It is worth remembering that such means of publicity need to sell a large number of tickets to justify their cost.

Your biggest expenditure will be in the form of royalties, and this is one item there is no way round. There are, of course, a great many plays now out of copyright: Greek classics, Restoration comedies, Shakespeare, Oscar Wilde, and so on, but as these will require expenditure on costumes, it's very much a matter of what you gain on the swings. But to get back to royalties; the amount you have to pay will depend on how many performances you intend to give and there is usually a sliding scale of fees so that the more performances, the less you pay *pro rata*. Again, if your maximum possible audience is very small you can sometimes get a lower rate of royalty agreed by the publishers or copyright holders. The main thing to bear in mind is that royalties have to be paid in advance before a licence to perform the selected play is given. Where and to whom the amount payable should be sent is to be found in the first few pages of your play copy.

Few societies are lucky enough to own their own premises, so that a hall will have to be hired and again often paid for in advance with the possibility of supplementary charges for electricity used and for heating. Many such halls that I have seen contain no lighting equipment suitable for dramatic productions, so you may either have to buy or hire a dimmer board and several spotlights. Strand Electric, who supply the majority of professional theatres with equipment, have an enormous hire department and are able to supply just about everything you could conceivably need. Don't leave this side of a production until the last moment, or you may be unlucky. Order your requirements well in advance, and bear in mind that you will also need to pay a substantial deposit.

The same applies to costumes, and here I cannot recommend you too strongly to get your orders in well in advance. The major costume-hire houses these days have such large, regular commitments to television that you may well find the items you need are out of stock.

Finally, earmark a substantial part of your budget for sundry items such as paint, timber, screws and nails. The bill for these commodities can run to several pounds and despite economic use and careful hoarding from production to production I have always found that many items have to be bought anew each time. By the way, remember that somebody has to pay for the coffee and biscuits consumed during rehearsals!

The reason that I have listed all these things in some detail is that they all have to be paid for before you have any form of income from your production. The cost can be assessed fairly accurately, so you can work out how much you will need to put on a play and then decide how you are going to set about raising the necessary funds. What you cannot work out much in advance, unfortunately, is the income from your efforts, for it is seldom safe to assume that you will sell every seat for every performance. One point that springs to mind in this connection if you are planning on open-air production is the advisability of taking out a Pluvius insurance policy. For a fixed premium this will guarantee you against a total loss of gate-money in the event of a performance being rained off, and this can go a long way towards taking the sting out of a substantial costume bill.

As your society becomes established, the financial side of things will in some respects get easier. You will probably build up a supply of scenery, a wardrobe, and a certain amount of lighting equipment of your own. You will also begin to know your audience and therefore be able to assess more accurately how many you are likely to attract to your performances. But always set a budget for a production so that the producer may know exactly how much he can spend. It is then up to him to cut corners if necessary to stay within that budget.

Chapter 2

The Producer

Is it an advantage for a drama producer to have been an actor? Well that's a question that can give rise to endless discussion and numerous celebrated examples can be found in the professional theatre to support the argument either way. An experienced actor is perhaps more aware of the special problems of his art and will therefore not ask other actors to do things he couldn't do himself, but on the other hand the non-acting producer may be better able to assess a scene or a performance from an audience point of view. I think it more important that any producer, whatever his background, should study the psychology of his cast: that he should be sympathetically aware of each individual's difficulties and nervous tensions.

Can anyone learn to be a producer? There I think the answer is a categorical 'yes'. Although much of the job is a matter of instinct and sensitivity, of feel for theatre, these are all aspects which develop with experience. But you also need to know how to set about the mechanics of production. However you interpret a particular play, there are certain things that always ought to be done to bring about the most efficient transfer from written word to live performance on stage. If you are about to produce a play for the very first time, I'm sure that if you work hard along the principles outlined in this chapter you will not find the task too daunting.

I can't stress too strongly that the best results always stem from the most thorough preparation. A finished performance should already have taken place in the producer's mind's eye before he peare's dialogue to sort out business in their own words, the emotion of the part stayed with Roger, while Alec could turn it off instantly like a tap and immediately become himself. By the end of the afternoon, the scenes were set to their mutual satisfaction and indeed became highlights of the play in performance, yet both actors had followed quite different courses to arrive at that end product.

Having said all that, there are of course several constants, such as make-up, voice production, and so on, the rudiments of which will be dealt with later in this book. The purpose of this chapter is to try to pass on to you some of the elements of acting which I hope I have learned over twenty-five years. It is your privilege to disagree with them. I can only say that they have worked for me and for others who have acted under my direction. One dictum bears repeating because I submit that it is indisputable: it is that the only way to learn about acting is to act. Reading and thinking about it can help, but practical experience remains the finest teacher.

The first thing to do with any part is to read and re-read the play over and over again. Not just the scenes which involve the character you are playing, but the whole play. Depending on the kind of memory you have you will probably find that the dialogue starts to become familiar, but at this stage don't make any conscious effort to learn your lines by heart. At the first reading, your producer will perhaps have given you an outline of how he sees your character, but the interpretation will develop through your own reading and through his early rehearsals. If you are word-perfect too soon, your lines will be coloured by inflexions and cadences which do not spring from character analysis and, having once been acquired that way, they are doubly difficult to eradicate.

In this repeated reading of the play, what should you be looking for in particular? Well, first and foremost, the character you are to play will most likely not only be defined by what that character says himself, but by what other characters in the play say about him. Look for every reference you can find, wherever it occurs, even if these references conflict. Let us assume, for example, that you were studying the character of Anthony in *Anthony and Cleopatra*. You will find that he reveals much about himself in his own speeches, but very different slants on him are given in speeches by Cleopatra, Enobarbus and Caesar, among others. Obviously no single assessment of him is complete in itself, but the truth lies in an amalgam of all the descriptions.

Once you think you are fairly well acquainted with the personality that you hope to convey, you must start to think of ways in which you might be able to put these facets across. Where you start will depend entirely on you and will vary from actor to actor. For instance, that fine character actress Beryl Reid always says that she starts from the feet. She tries to imagine how her character would walk, or stand, and once she has got that right, all the other characteristics begin to fall into place. Sir Laurence Oliver has been quoted as saying that the first thing he tries to find is a voice that fits the character, and indeed this would seem to be borne out by the widely differing sounds he produced, for instance, in his portrayals of Richard III and Othello. Whichever course you discover suits you best, you will find one thing to be true: when you have settled on any one major characteristic to your own satisfaction, then all the others do tend to come much more easily. I don't know why this should be so, but it is something I have always found does happen in practice.

In my opinion, the best time to start to learn lines accurately by heart is immediately after the producer has set the play. In other words, in all probability after about the third rehearsal. My reason for this is that you will then be able to learn words and moves together as an integrated whole, and indeed I know many actors who find it totally impossible to learn words without the moves and actions to go with them. Furthermore, all subsequent rehearsals will be largely a waste of your own and your producer's time if you continue to read your part. There are countless other details to be absorbed and this will not be easy if the lines are not coming to mind without effort.

From here on, development will be worked out mainly between the individual actor and producer and will obviously vary from play to play, but there are still many things that you can do in your own private study between rehearsals. For example, always look for opportunities to vary your pace of delivery, not only from scene to scene, but perhaps even more important, within the body of a single speech. This is the aspect which brings realism to dialogue. Try listening to a conversation in which you are not taking part, not so much for the significance of content, but for the very clear sound patterns that emerge. Notice how some phrases are, as it were, tucked away in parenthesis and considerably speeded up, so that main points are slowed down and emphasised. Listen to the way in which one speaker will raise the pitch of his voice to cap the tone of the preceding speaker, in order to arrest attention. Observe how a person will sometimes repeat the first word, or two words, of a sentence, quite deliberately as another ear-catcher. While I do not generally advocate taking gross liberties with the author's written word, this sort of trick seems to be totally permissible. Of course, a writer with a real ear for naturalistic dialogue – such as Pinter for example – will have incorporated such characteristics in the first place. However, having yourself got the feeling for these shifting sound patterns, go back to the printed words of your play and you will find how differently the written dialogue leaps at you from the page. Always try to avoid catching exactly the intonation of the previous speaker, which is one of the easiest things to do and a common fault in amateur performances. This tends to flatten everything out into a boring monotone which will lose an audience's attention more quickly than anything. It may be that a particular exchange of dialogue *should* be dull, monotonous and boring, for a specific dramatic effect, but this only your producer can decide.

There should come a point, fairly late in rehearsals, when your performance is pretty well fixed. You will have tried different delivery of lines and so on, and arrived at the most effective and workable way of doing things. I hope your producer will be able to tell you when he thinks your performance is exactly right. From that point on, don't attempt any radical changes, for they will undermine your own confidence and worry your fellow-actors who will not know what to expect. Rehearsals are the time for improvisation – performances are not. The West End professional, after a run of six months, might fairly be expected to cope with such things, but the average amateur, after a run of two nights, shouldn't have to.

At this point, two general comments would seem to be pertinent. If your producer, from the beginning, can be seen to have done his own preparation thoroughly, it is always wisest to rely on his judgement even if you do not agree with it. Remember that he is in the best position to see exactly what you are doing on stage both as an individual and as a member of a team. A strange thing about acting is that you may often feel you are sounding or moving in a particular way, yet your performance is not coming over in that manner to an observer. It is also a curious fact that, at some stage in your acting career, you are pretty certain to be seized by an almost irresistible desire to *ad lib*, to 'gag', to introduce 'in' jokes. Please, don't do it. If I had to stipulate just one thing that it is always wrong for an actor to do in any play, that would be it. I'm not talking about revues and pantomimes, which are rather different, but even in those spheres the funniest and apparently spontaneous comedians, such as Morecambe and Wise, Frankie Howerd and Ronnie Corbett, usually rehearse their '*ad libs*' to the last detail. I recently worked with an actor who told me with great glee that in his previous production he had gagged one scene every night. 'Poor old Bob never knew what to expect,' he gloated. 'I said something different at every performance, and just swept off to leave him roasting.' He didn't seem to realise that he had also left his audience roasting. I told him that if I caught him doing it just once, he would be out of that cast so fast his feet wouldn't touch.

Another fundamental aspect about dialogue which perhaps I should have mentioned earlier is that it is at all times important to learn the *meaning* of your lines and not just to absorb them parrot-fashion. If this precept is followed two wonderful things cannot help but follow: in performance, your speeches will sound miraculously spontaneous as though you really had just thought of them for the first time, and secondly the audience will receive the thoughts rather than the words. I recently watched impressive performances, in contemporary plays, by those illustrious knights Sir Ralph Richardson and Sir Alec Guinness, and on both occasions came away from the theatre with a very clear recollection of certain lines. On subsequently reading the plays, I found I had absorbed very clearly the import of those lines, although they had been expressed in fact with quite different words. To carry this moral a stage further, I was once required to produce an amateur company in *Macbeth*. We had longer than usual to rehearse and so, as an experiment, I spent a couple of weeks with the cast getting them to paraphrase all their lines, analysing them, and translating them into modern language. We then went back to Shakespeare's text and proceeded in the normal manner. On the first night, a professional producer in the audience told me that it was the first time he had seen a production of *Macbeth* in which he *felt* as though he understood every word that was spoken.

This matter of thought process in dialogue leads me to the next subject, which is the memorising of lines. I am constantly asked by young newcomers to the stage, and indeed by audience members, whether there are any tricks of the trade when it comes to learning. They seem to believe that there is a great mystique about this part of acting or that those who practise it have unusual brain powers. I cannot accept either of these premises, because those who say they 'Couldn't ever do it' have probably never tried, and certainly many of the best actors I know would scarcely rate as highly intelligent in other fields.

First, let it be said that there are no short cuts to memorising. For most of us it is sheer hard work. There are indeed people with photographic memories and as a young actor in repertory I once possessed this faculty myself. It was only necessary to read a play through once, and I had total recall of the part I was playing: I could actually see the printed page in my mind's eye as I recited the lines. It was an advantage when learning a different role every week, but I think a disadvantage towards the real in-depth study of character. After several years spent in radio, where pretty well everything was read from scripts, the 'gift' faded and I no longer have it.

I have already advocated constant reading of the whole play with which you are concerned and this is equally important when it comes to learning lines. It is a grave mistake to acquire simply the last few words of the previous speakers' lines as a cue, for you will find in practice that those 'last few words' don't always come out, and you will be left high and dry waiting for a cue that never arrives.

One actor who has appeared in many of my productions has a learning method of his own that I have never tried personally, but it seems to work for him. First of all he makes a tape recording of the whole play, and then plays it back reciting his own lines as they come up. Then he makes another tape with only the other characters' speeches, leaving gaps for his own. This means in effect that he can undertake word rehearsals on his own whenever he chooses. There must be few these days who neither own nor have access to a tape recorder, so I pass on the system for what it's worth.

There are a few memory tricks that you may find useful, and to illustrate how they might be employed, let me relate them to a specific example. Not long ago, purely as an exercise, I set out to learn the part of John Aubrey in Patrick Garland's one-man play, *Brief Lives*. In this, the character is on stage alone for a matter of two hours, reminiscing in seemingly haphazard vein about the acquaintances and experiences of a lifetime. The text is sprinkled with names and dates, and succeeding stories seem to bear little or no relation to each other – at least that was the impression I gained when seeing Roy Dotrice perform the play on stage. It did look like a super-human, well-nigh impossible task. But let us see how different a picture emerges when one begins to study the text.

First, the old man is roused from his bed by the sounds of drunks and carriages in the street, a baby crying in the next room, and someone hammering in the chamber above. These prompt him to grumble about the dissoluteness of the times, to describe his physical surroundings, setting the scene as one room in a lodging house, and to remember his own childhood. This was marred by sickness, and the recollection sets him to remembering anecdotes about doctors and primitive cures. He also has a long speech about the superstitions prevalent during his childhood. From there it is a natural step to his schooldays, and this sparks off a dissertation on his own 'idea for the education of a young gentleman' which he has written, and carries him on to university, and the personalities he met there. Then there occurs a fairly abrupt change as he remembers details of the civil war, and so on through to the restoration, and as the first act ends he is just building up to memories of the execution of Raleigh as he drops off to sleep in his chair before the fire.

You will see from the foregoing that there is a very distinct pattern of thought process, with nearly every section leading logically to the next. Once the broad outline has been grasped, the details and individual stories the character tells fall more readily into place. However, I did find two moments which just would not stick in my mind. One was during his description of his theory for education. He reads lines from his pamphlet, and then expands on them to the audience, and at one point he is talking about the evils of ale houses but the merits of taverns. The benefits of wine include the fact that it 'is acknowledged to be a good medicine against the worms.' The next line from his pamphlet is, 'No scholar to rise too early.' This was a completely blind spot for me, until I added in my mind the thought process – 'medicine against the worms' – the *early* bird catches the worm – 'No scholar to rise too *early*'. Not Aubrey's thought process, to be sure, but it helped me.

The other difficult moment came when Aubrey finishes talking about his college president, Dr. Ralph Kettell, and then goes on in general terms about the civil war, starting, 'In 1642, war thundered.' That date would not stay in my mind, until I observed that at the end of the previous speech there was an effects cue for a street-crier calling 'new mackerel – new mackerel – new – new.' And suddenly it clicked. The rhyming sound of 'new' and 'two', immediately gave me 1642.

Now take those two instances out of that specific context and you will see that they could be applied in a variety of situations. You may often find, in any play, that there is one line that just will not stay in your mind. Dream up some fantastic image, bizarre if you like, relate the picture in your mind with the words in question and you may well find that the problem has vanished. The other trick, of a rhyming association, may not be so generally useful but it is worth bearing in mind.

I think it is also true that memory improves with use, and you can perform exercises in the same way that a musician will play scales. I don't suggest that you rush off immediately and try to learn *Brief Lives*, but here is a simple routine which can also be used as a fairly impressive party trick. Make up a list of objects, say twenty in number, of which you can instantly call to mind a clear mental picture. I find it best if the name of the object rhymes loosely with the number, thus: one, gun; two, shoe; three, bee, etc. Then ask friends to give you another list of twenty objects, and as they name each one, relate a mental image of that object with the picture already in your mind for that number. Suppose they gave you a sailing ship, (you might picture a ship with a cannon set up in its bows), a bus (see in your mind's eye an enormous shoe, with wheels and windows in the side) and a bicycle, (a bee riding a bike?). In every case, the more outlandish the combined image, the more readily it will stay in mind. After you have the full twenty, recite the full list back to them, in order, then backwards, then ask them to name any number and tell them the object they named. If your assistant says, 'two', for example, your thought process will be, 'two – shoe,' and then you will find you get a clear picture of that shoe with wheels and windows, and immediately you will remember 'bus.' I have found that with a little effort I have been able to do this with a list of forty objects.

Forgive me the foregoing digression but I have found the mental exercise I have described an amusing way of oiling the wheels of memory, and it could just possibly be of help to some of you.

As I have said elsewhere, suggestions for make-up, voice-training and speech and movement will be dealt with in subsequent chapters of this book. Indeed, the really dedicated amateur actor will probably want to acquire as much knowledge as possible about all aspects of theatre and I hope he will find something of interest in every chapter, but there are just a few more general points that I think we might usefully talk about here.

I hope that you will not always be involved in modern plays, but will from time to time be cast in period, costume works. They do present special problems of their own, not least of which is learning to move on stage convincingly in clothes which you are unaccustomed to wearing. Most likely your society will be hiring costumes and these will not be available until just before performance, which is far too late for you to feel at home in them. It is therefore essential, from an early stage of rehearsal, to provide yourself with something similar that will hamper, or restrict, your freedom of movement in the same way that your costume will. One of my teachers told me of an experience which emphasises this point. He had to wear a costume with riding breeches, boots and spurs, and his first entrance was at the top of an enormous flight of stairs. He did not get the spurs until the first performance when, starting to descend the stairs, his heel caught on the first tread and sent him base over apex to the bottom. Up to that point, the play had not been a farce! However, he quickly learned that to come down stairs in spurs, it is necessary to adopt a slightly sideways stance to give clearance. On another occasion, this same actor had to open a door for a lady in a full length, flowing skirt, and follow her off stage. The scene had always been rehearsed in modern clothes, and he had not discovered the necessity of allowing a pause before following the lady. When costumes were worn for the first time, he started his exit smartly after her, trod on her skirt, and ripped it badly. Had she been wearing a practice skirt at rehearsals, this disaster would never have occurred. So if the men in your play are going to be dressed in tights, let them have ample rehearsal in such garments. Tights are now readily and cheaply available, and you will find that without the disguise of relatively loose trousers, you will become much more aware of your legs, and how you stand, sit and walk.

The same thing applies to the use of everyday articles which you may have to handle in a scene: bottles, glasses, cups and saucers, and so on. These are things we use in our daily lives without thinking about it, but you will find that when you come to use them in the artificial situation of a play, while speaking someone else's words that you have learned, the natural ease of familiarity will disappear unless you rehearse, *with* the props, over and over again. There is a marvellous scene in *Charley's Aunt*, in which Fanny Babbs, as the phoney aunt, pours out cups of tea and, while speaking to the character on one side of him, pours tea and milk, on the other side, into Mr. Spettigrew's top hat. Not a common occurrence, I agree, but on stage it must look spontaneous and easy. From personal experience, I can tell you that it may take the better part of a whole rehearsal, with all the props, to get the timing exactly right.

Finally, I would urge you to be at all times, during rehearsal, fully physically aware of yourself. When you are struggling for words, this will be difficult, but as the lines grow more familiar, try to think what you are doing with your hands and arms, of how you are standing, or sitting. How many times I have seen a performance with good vocal delivery marred by painfully contorted limbs, with hands unnaturally clasped, or, worse, thrust into pockets. I once had a young man appearing in his very first play, in which he had just one long speech. All I required was that he should stand fairly still, looking elegantly relaxed. By degrees we got him almost there, when I suddenly noticed that he was waggling an index finger, beating time to his words on his thigh. The result was ludicrous, and quite hypnotic to an audience, totally distracting attention from what he was saying. Relaxation on stage is of paramount importance, and is something I shall write about later on.

Chapter 5
Lighting

On one occasion when I was visiting the sales department of a firm of theatre-lighting manufacturers, the young man in front of me in the queue said to the assistant, 'We're putting on a pantomime, and we want our Demon King to look green. Have you got any green bulbs?' Although that may raise a smile from those who know something about stage-lighting, to the totally uninitiated it must seem to be a very reasonable question.

There are, admittedly, several well-established amateur theatres throughout the country with enviable equipment and accomplished people to operate it. This chapter is not addressed to them. But I have found by observation that the majority of small groups fall into two classes: there are those, often found in schools, endowed with quite sophisticated lighting units that they don't know how to use, and there are those with no equipment of their own who have to make do with the often pitifully inadequate equipment in the halls that they hire.

Perhaps it would be useful to point out at this stage that all halls licensed for public performances have to abide, rightly and properly, by stringent fire-precaution regulations. A member of the local Fire Service is quite likely to turn up the night before your play opens to make sure that everything on the stage is fireproof, and I do mean everything, such as curtains, furniture and so on. You would be well advised to see that it is, too, for your visitor is empowered to stop the performance if he finds anything amiss. Now the reason for including this information in a chapter on lighting is that in the electrical circuitry of a hall we have perhaps the most palpable potential fire-raiser. When booking the hall in the first place, the secretary should make enquiries about the maximum load that the electric power supply is capable of taking. This will, to a large extent, dictate the number of spotlights or at least the total amount of power which can be used, and that information is essential before a lighting plot can be worked out.

Now maybe the play you are hoping to present calls for the use of naked flame in some form or other, such as a torch, candle, brazier, or gas-fire and so on. Please do check out at an early stage how the introduction of any of these items would be affected by the existing fire regulations. It is always possible to substitute alternatives, but the sooner you know where you stand the better.

Next perhaps we might take a look at some of the hardware you are going to need to light your play adequately.

I have always been a staunch advocate of acquiring one's own equipment and gradually building this up over the years, because in this way a producer will know at the outset of a production exactly what he can and cannot achieve with the resources at his disposal. Even if he is not a technical man himself, a basic lighting plot should be a fundamental part of his initial planning, and not something that is stuck on afterwards. So, let us consider first of all the sort of items you are going to need even for simple illumination.

A dimmer board of some description is to my mind an absolute essential, and will probably prove to be the most expensive item on the list. Where resources are severely limited, I should recommend hiring a board at least for the first few productions, until you have managed to build up a bank account. Strand Electric are undoubtedly the best-known suppliers in England and they can provide a model called the Junior, which has eight separate channels. This means that you can have independent control over either eight separate lights, or eight groups of lights and these can be faded in or out, slowly or quickly, as required. For many years now I have been extremely lucky to have as a lighting man an electronics engineer who invented and built a control panel of remarkably small dimensions which can cope with up to thirty-six channels. These are sub-divided into six separate units, which can be pre-set to a desired effect, each of them linked to one fader. The whole thing is easily portable, and we have used it in our own very small theatre, in large school halls and in the open air. The cost of making this board was greatly below that of purchasing a far less versatile unit, and I strongly urge any new group to make painstaking enquiries among family, friends and acquaintances to see if they can find an electrician capable of making them a board.

Perhaps some of you will have had experience of appearing in a hall with nothing more than, say, a couple of normal domestic type lights suspended above the stage, operated from a switch panel in the wings. Indeed, plays *can* be presented in such circumstances, but as I said at the outset, the purpose of this book is to suggest ways in which we can aim at optimum standards of production. Let me tell you a story which underlines my own insistence on the need for a dimmer board.

I was once a member of a small professional company which toured all over the country appearing in schools, colleges and art clubs, with a mixed programme of mime, illustrated lectures on the history of theatre and one-act plays. We performed in places where there were stages with curtains, places with one or the other, and in some places with neither. The closing item in the first half of the programme was usually a Harlequinade at the end of which the four principal characters perched themselves on stools at the back of the acting area, and waited either for a curtain or a black-out to make their exit. At one school we were asked to perform in the gymnasium under their ordinary lights, without stage or curtain. The only way of effecting a black-out was by throwing a master switch some distance away at the end of a corridor. We worked out a plan whereby a prefect standing in the doorway of the gym would signal to another prefect at the switch as we sat on our stools. Switch prefect would then plunge us all into darkness, count ten to allow us to creep off with our stools, and then put the lights on again. Now perhaps it was this young lady's first theatrical 'experience', but I'm quite sure she has never counted to ten so quickly before or since. We sat on our stools, the lights went out as pre-arranged, and to our horror came on again almost immediately, revealing four pathetic little actors, all creeping off in most undignified manner with stools under their arms. In retrospect it is funny, of course, but at the time it felt like the most embarrassing moment of our lives.

You need a dimmer board!

Where do we need to place the lights that are operated from that board? This is determined entirely by what those lights are required to do. Their primary function is to illuminate the actors, especially their faces, for the most subtle and potentially gripping performance will not be much use if the audience cannot see it. It is virtually impossible to illuminate faces satisfactorily with a light source from one direction only, for as those faces move about the stage they will from time to time be obscured by shadows thrown by other actors or pieces of scenery, or even by parts of their own bodies. Those overhead domestic lights I mentioned in an earlier paragraph are disastrous, because the forehead will cast shadow over the eyes, the nose will shadow the mouth, and so on, defeating any known method of make-up, as will be seen in a later chapter.

For very much the same reason, footlights are seldom, if ever, used these days. They may be introduced for a special effect, or to give the impression of a stage within the stage, as for example during the music-hall comedian scenes by Archie Rice in *The Entertainer*. The same idea was used in the Broadway production of the musical show *Gypsy* (I didn't see the London presentation) for scenes in which Rose was supposed to be appearing in a strip show. The result is just the reverse of those overhead lights, with shadows thrown the opposite way, and the effect on a face can be garish and bizarre – most dramatic in the examples I have cited, but quite out of place in the majority of plays.

So we arrive at the conclusion that actors are best lit, primarily, from spots placed facing the stage and known as FOH (Front Of House) spots. These may be mounted on a transverse beam in the auditorium, or on a specially mounted lighting bar; they may be placed on stands at the sides of the theatre, or perhaps fixed on the side walls. The best effects will be achieved, with any of these alternatives, if the spots are directed to cast their beams at an angle across the stage, so that those placed on the left hand side of the auditorium, facing the stage, are aimed at the right hand side of the stage, and vice versa. For a fairly small hall or theatre you will probably find that you will need from four to six of these spots and they should preferably be of a kind with variable focus so that the projected beam can cover either a very narrow or very wide area, as required. It is perhaps worth pointing out in this connection that once the focus of a spot has been established, then its use is restricted to such limitations for the duration of the performance. Let us suppose that the producer wants to play a scene with the stage blacked out, save for one narrow spot lighting only the head and shoulders of an actor: then he will, by tying up one of his spots for just that effect, reduce the number available for overall illumination. That may seem obvious, but producers often tend to forget such factors, as my own lighting technician frequently reminds me!

In addition to the FOH lighting, you will need some units *on* stage as well, either suspended overhead in the flies, set directly underneath a cyclorama, or placed in the wings. In practice, we have found the most versatile items to be a couple of four-feet long battens, each housing four separate lamps, linked in pairs alternately. These do not throw a beam, but use bulbs seated in reflectors, thereby giving a diffused light, the colour of which can be changed by use of gelatines. Fairly satisfactory results can be achieved with the few lighting units listed so far, but doubtless as you progress you will feel the need to add other items, such as fixed focus spots and so on, and however much you acquire it is only fair to warn you that you are never likely to feel that you have enough.

If the stage you use is a fairly deep one, the FOH spots will leave lots of areas in shadow and it will be desirable to mount rows of battens above the stage, not mounted to light directly downwards, for reasons already explained, but with spots angled at say forty-five degrees, so that from just behind the curtain line you can light centre stage, and from a second batten half-way back you can light to the rear of the stage.

When working out your lighting plot always consider the apparent sources of light from the audience point of view. If a door is opened onto a hall or another room, then light must be seen to spill onto the stage from that room, so you will need a spot or a flood off-stage at that point. There may be a window through which the stage is lit by sun or moon and you will need off-stage lights there as well. Where practical lights are used on stage, such as a reading lamp, or a candle, the actual light may not always be enough to give the desired effect and will therefore have to be amplified by facing in one of your spots focused on the area.

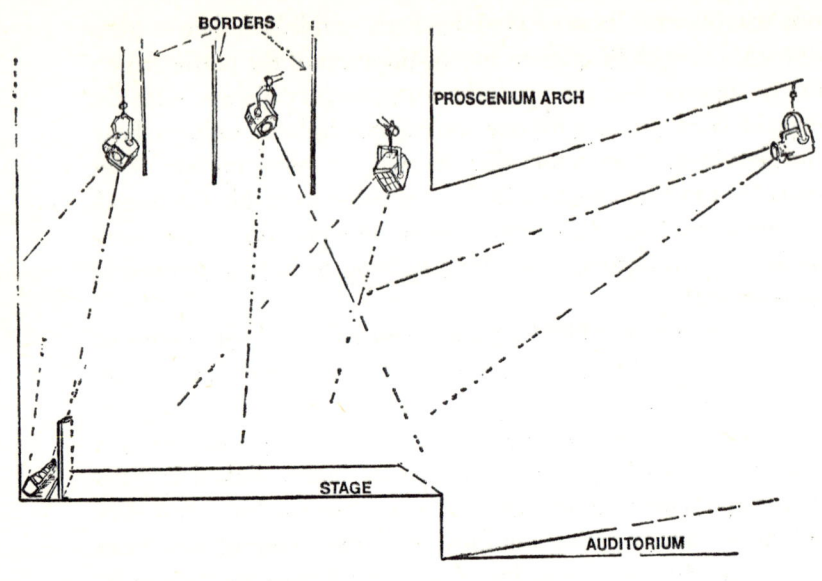

Fig. 3 Basic lighting installation

The next thing to consider is which areas of the stage are the main acting areas. After he has set his moves, the producer will be able to specify certain parts of the stage in which most of the action takes place and these can be shown by circles drawn on a scale plan. Even when full daylight lighting is called for, it is wise to throw more concentrated illumination on these principal areas although the distinction can be subtle and not obtrusively obvious to the audience.

Finally there is the matter of the colours you use in your lights. There is a tremendously wide range of coloured gelatines available, all designated by numbers, and purchased in large sheets which you must then cut to the size of the frames which fit your spots and battens. You will certainly need a range of blues, from a very pale steel to dark blue; a selection of ambers; some pink to add warmth to your FOH lights; red if you need to simulate firelight, and other colours for special effects can be obtained as and when required. Our novice at the beginning of this chapter obviously needed a sheet of green.

Just as the focus of your FOH lights has to remain for the duration of performance, so does any colour you place in them, thereby further limiting their use. I have seen amateur theatres in which the spots were accessible out of sight of the audience, and could be changed during a show, but this is most unusual. So, colour changes really have to be affected through your off-stage lights. For example, those four lamp battens I have described could have, say, ambers in compartments one and three and blues in two and four and, placed outside a window, or under a cyclorama, will provide you with day or night effects as required.

The bane of all stage lighting is the unwanted shadow, which can kill the credibility of the most beautiful effects. To give you an example, let us suppose that we have a scene in which the cyclorama is in full view as a clear blue sky and that just below this there is a terrace with a low balustrade wall. Unless the intensity of light from various areas is properly balanced, the strong FOH spots may well project in outline the shadow of that balustrade on the 'sky', shattering the illusion. The shadows of the actors will also work in the same way of course. To some extent this undesirable effect can be eliminated by side lighting, directed onto the cyclorama and killing the shadows.

There are some aspects of lighting, like acting, about which one can be quite dogmatic. There are definite 'do's' and 'don'ts'. But for the most part, like acting, it is open to discussion and experimentation to find the best methods for any given situation. Unfortunately, for most amateur groups there is never enough time to experiment with light placing, and this is why I repeat the essential need for the lighting technician and the scenic designer or builders to work in close consulation with the producer at the planning stage of a production.

To conclude this chapter on the basic elements of lighting, I should like to cover a few of the special requirements for open-air productions.

The first thing to bear in mind is the distance that you will almost certainly have to cover with your lights. An ideal garden setting may well give you an acting area of something like sixty feet by thirty, which is about the size of the stage at Covent Garden where they have a total power supply of two megawatts, which you are scarcely likely to have at your disposal.

When setting up your equipment there are three main aspects to consider, and these are (1) the acting area (2) the background, and (3) the audience area, all to be dealt with individually.

First, then, the acting area. However many spots you have available, try to mount them as high as possible. They could be placed in trees, but a good practical idea is to set up tall poles guy-roped to the ground for firmness. Slide movable sleeves over these poles and attach them to ropes passed over pulleys at the top of the poles. By attaching your spots to these sleeves, they can then be raised and lowered for adjustments and colour changes, without perching precariously on ladders.

Although I have suggested that footlights are unnecessary for indoor work it is almost essential for the open-air production to obtain a set of floodlights which should be placed at ground level on the edge of your acting area. These will counteract to some extent the shadows from your high spots and will also fill in areas which the spots do not cover.

Next, the background. Whether or not you are using constructed pieces of scenery you will almost certainly want to take advantage of natural features, such as hedges, shrubberies, or bushes. These will not be sufficiently illuminated by your spots, so try to cover them with separate floods, using coloured gelatines to add interest.

Finally, the audience area. Strings of coloured lights are perhaps the most attractive means of lighting the 'auditorium', and these should be connected to the dimmer board so that they can be faded out when the action commences. Incidentally, remember that in the open air your stage lights have to fill the function of a curtain and have to be faded right down to suggest the passing of time and to denote the ends of scenes and acts. In practice I have always found it best to use all the lights right from the beginning, even though this may be in daylight, for as darkness falls and the lights slowly begin to take effect the result is magical and beautiful.

In conclusion it is worth bearing in mind that whatever your indoor cable requirements are, you can reckon on multiplying those requirements by four for the greater distances to be covered outside. All connections should be put inside plastic bags, to stop water from any source getting in. At the end of each performance turn your floodlights face downwards and cover your dimmer board with a waterproof sheet. If you are the lighting man, when operating the board it is a worthwhile safety precaution to wear gum-boots.

I have refrained throughout from using the technical names and code numbers of lighting components, because these do tend to change slightly as time goes by and occasional developments are introduced. Prices, too, seemed pointless as these will doubtless fluctuate considerably. However, if this chapter has given you a rudimentary idea of basic essentials, lighting-suppliers or hirers will be able to tell you exactly which items you need for each purpose. This is unquestionably the most expensive aspect of production for any new group starting out, but time, trouble and money well spent will equally unquestionably enhance your performances.

Chapter 6

Costumes and Scenery

It may seem surprising that I have chosen to combine in one chapter two subjects that could each involve years of study. The would-be designer should learn as much as possible about the history of costume and a broad knowledge of architectural styles is also an asset. There are, of course, many excellent books on these matters and it would be impossible to condense all this information into a few pages. My purpose is rather to suggest, by means of several examples, ways in which costumes and scenery can be approached imaginatively and inexpensively. Anyone who undertakes amateur production will discover, sooner or later, that he is required to give guidance in those areas and may very well have to lend manual assistance as well. I don't think I have ever directed a play without having to spend several hours wielding screw-driver and paint brush.

One basic quality that a producer should endeavour to achieve with any play is a uniformity of style. If realism is to be the keynote, then it must extend to sets, costumes and acting, while if an impressionist effect is desired then that too should be common to all three. How often one sees productions marred because the conventions have been mixed!

When we started a small amateur theatre of our own some years ago, our very slender resources had soon been totally absorbed by the installation of seating, basic lighting equipment as described in the previous chapter, a fairly elaborate sound system which will be dealt with later on, and a set of neutral-coloured drapes across the wings and the back of the stage. We therefore chose as our first play a two-hander by Arnold Wesker called *Four Seasons* which is set in a decaying, deserted house. The two characters, Adam and Beatrice, arrive in winter, set up home in the house and live there for a year, finally leaving it, very much as they found it, in autumn. Our scenery consisted of an irregularly shaped door frame, free-standing, and a window frame suspended on strips of perforated metal from the flies. The only furniture used was a small plain table, two kitchen chairs, one with a broken back, and a small wooden chest. At the beginning of the play the window frame was draped with a tattered length of grey muslin. Throughout the action, small details were changed in each scene. The muslin was replaced with new-looking curtains, the broken chair was 'mended' and replaced by a similar chair painted a brighter colour. Flowers were introduced in the Spring scene, and dead leaves in the autumn. The change of season was mainly reflected in the costumes, sweaters and slacks throughout, but in shades of green for spring, gold for summer and deep, dark browns for the autumn. No attempt was made at realism in the lighting, but again the colours used suggested the seasons, and during the frequent long soliloquies which occur in the play, the actor concerned was lit by a single, tight spot, while the rest of the stage was almost in darkness. The only other thing we had to make was a sound effects tape which carried our music and the sounds associated with the various seasons, such as wind, bird song, and so on. This extremely low-budget production was a considerable financial success and provided us with funds for more elaborate scenery for the following presentation. It would doubtless have been possible to present *Four Seasons* with no scenery at all, but I believe that this approach is asking a great deal of any audience. Our two basic pieces provided focal points as the curtain went up and their deliberately irregular shapes immediately indicated the impressionist convention; they helped the audience settle straightway into a mood to accept the somewhat difficult dialogue, mime sequences, and the unrealistic lighting. There was, I hope, a uniformity of convention about the whole production.

This sort of technique can also be applied successfully to a larger-scale production with more elaborate costumes, though naturally the cost will be proportionately higher. On another

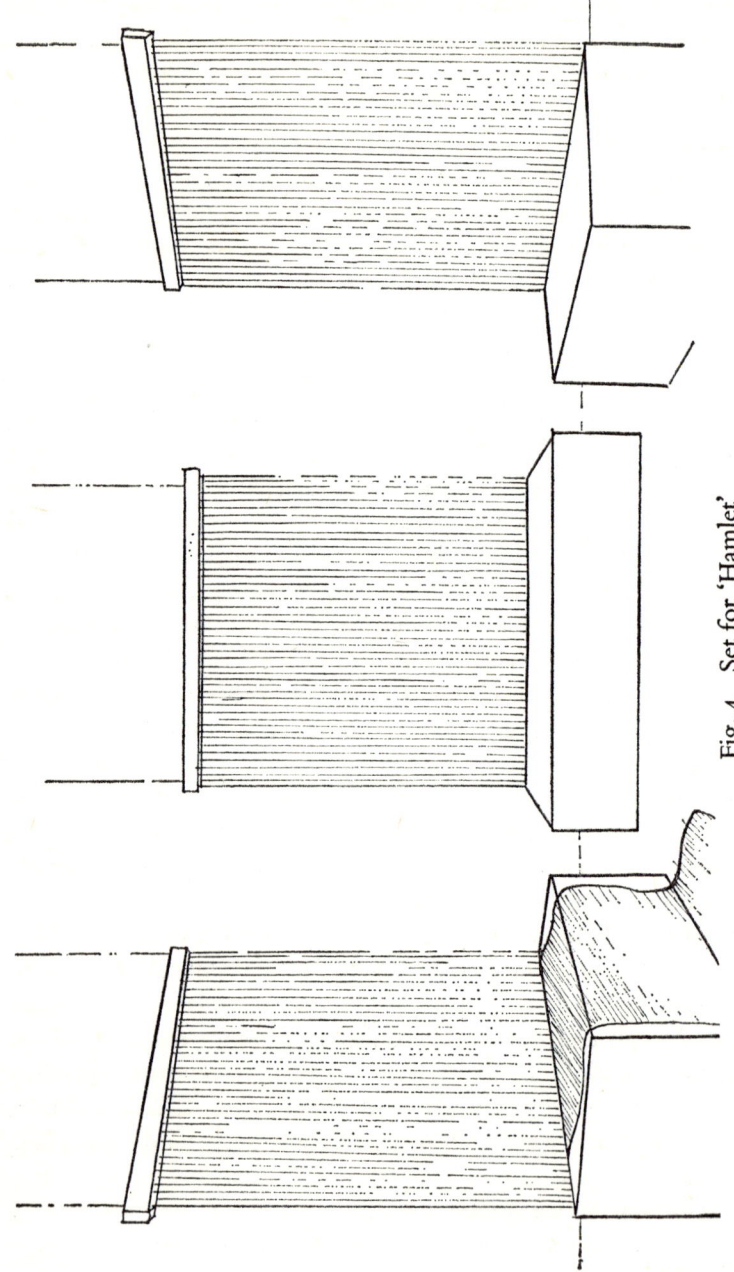

Fig. 4 Set for 'Hamlet'

occasion we wanted to mount a production of *Hamlet* to take on tour to schools. The first problem was to devise a set which would suit the numerous scenes inside and outside the castle at Elsinore, yet one that could be easily transported and set up in a matter of hours on stages of varying sizes. As it happens, the producer was also a brilliantly imaginative designer himself and solved the problem magnificently.

First, we made three collapsible rostra, each six feet long, eighteen inches high, and two feet wide. As actors were going to have to sit, stand and even fight on these rostra, they had to be of fairly substantial construction. We made stout timber frames, and solid planking tops which could be dropped into place and fixed with coach bolts held by wing nuts screwed on the inside. Fronts and sides were covered by hardboard, and the back left empty. These were then painted matt black and sprayed lightly in places with gold and bronze to give texture. One rostrum was set upstage, parallel with the back wall, and was used as the castle battlements in the opening, the King and Queen's throne in the council scene, and the stage for the players' scene. The other two were set up and down stage, parallel with the wings. One of them had a large sheet of green felt stowed underneath, with one edge tacked to the underside of the rostrum top. When pulled out and thrown completely over the rostrum it became the set for Ophelia's grave. Next we made three large screens, each six feet wide and some fifteen feet in height, consisting of a top and bottom batten, linked by lengths of thick twine spaced about two inches or less apart. When suspended from the flies, the heavy bottom batten kept the strings taught and it could also be rolled round to reduce the length of the strings to suit the height of the stage. The strings were also painted black and sprayed with gold in patches. One frame was set about a yard behind each rostrum, and assumed an entirely different aspect when lit from the front, the side, or behind. The only other piece we had to make was Ophelia's coffin, which was built to fit comfortably underneath the 'grave' rostrum. When it was in place, and the green felt returned to its original position, we were left with a plain black bench-type box for the final interior and the duel scene.

With such an impressionist set, we felt that it would be a mistake to have costumes that were clearly related to any specific

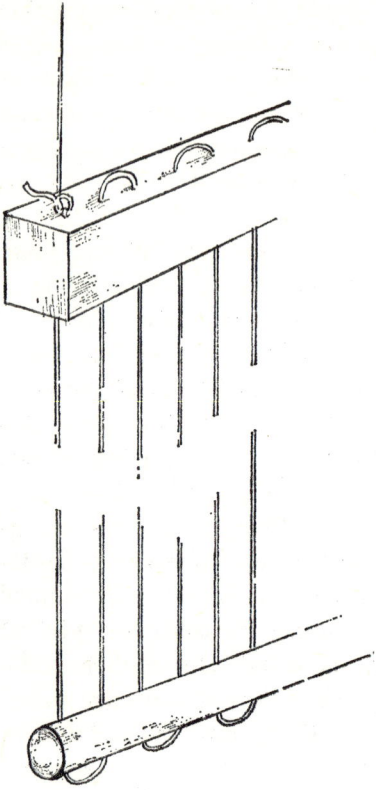

Fig. 5 'Hamlet' screens

period, yet we wanted a definite period *feel*. We therefore created our own conventions – for example, most of the men wore, not tights, but tightly fitting trousers and mid-calf length suede boots – and all the costumes were designed within those conventions. Again, we had uniformity of style. All our soldiers were dressed in black, with stiff felt tunics also sprayed lightly in bronze, giving the appearance of breast plates. Effective crowns were made for the King and Queen on wire frames with chunky pieces of cork, painted gold, and stuck with coloured stones. Amazingly durable, they are still in my wardrobe!

To anyone only acquainted with everyday dressmaking, it may seem strange to read of spraying and painting costumes for the stage, yet I assure you that wonderful effects can be achieved by this means. It is important to remember that dull, flat monotones are disastrous in drama, whether they occur in acting, scenery or costumes. With scenery and costumes, the one magic word to bear in mind at all times is 'texture'. Bold strokes, allied to good lighting give three-dimensional, dramatic results. We have on many occasions made marvellous costumes out of old sheets or cheap plain material, transformed by the use of brush-applied water-based paints or aerosol sprays. Even old suits can, on occasion, be made servicable by the application of a little paint.

To emphasise this point, and to underline the fact that such methods are not just make-do-and-mend tactics for impecunious amateurs, I may tell you I was once in an Old Vic production of *Henry V* designed by the now famous firm of Motley who used similar techniques to the full. At curtain up, the only things on stage were six huge poles: then soldiers entered and stood at the base of each one. As King Henry entered, the soldiers pulled cords, and from the audience it looked as though gloriously rich velvet banners cascaded down those poles. In fact, the banners were made of cheap, coarse canvas, bodly painted! Further, in this same production, all the English soldiers wore impressive red and blue parti-coloured tights, and these were made from an inexpensive job lot of army surplus arctic underwear, died half-red and half-blue. The King of France's mighty, flowing cloak was also made from canvas, hand painted and it looked beautiful (although it was rendered a little suspect on one occasion, as the King swept to centre stage, and a little brown mouse suddenly jumped from the folds and scampered off into the wings!).

I am aware that the examples I have given so far are all related to specific plays and therefore have no general application, but I hope they are making the point that an adventurous choice of plays by any society need not be hampered unduly by lack of space and funds. There are still a great many groups, unfortunately, who appear to select a play solely on the basis that it has more women than men in the cast and only one set. The very thought of scene-changes frightens them away from material which I am sure both they and their audiences would find more rewarding. It may seem impossible, at first glance, to build a solid looking set which can be changed radically without the aid of the elaborate machinery of a full-scale professional theatre, but let us see if this is strictly true.

I wanted to stage an open-air production of the historical

Fig. 6 The set for an open-air production of 'The Young Elizabeth'

costume drama *The Young Elizabeth*, which has scenes in various palaces and country houses and even a cell in the Tower. As we had considerable width to play with, we first of all built a stage made of rostra at three different heights, but linked to each other by steps. It was then possible to use the whole area for big scenes, and to concentrate action on just one of the rostra for smaller scenes, while the appearance of the other areas was changed. Behind the stage we built a symmetrical wall of flats, painted as stones, with three focal points, one behind each rostra or stage level. Now these focal points were, in fact, revolving flats with a plain stone wall painted on one side, and a wall with window on the other. In addition to this, we also made small cut-outs of

different shaped windows which could be hung on these flats out of view of the audience. Further, the entire centre stage section could be folded back and replaced by a practical door. As you will see, this gave us an enormous permutation of variations, all of which could be effected in a matter of seconds, often by the actor about to enter or just having left the stage.

I used the same basic idea for the construction of a piece of scenery for indoor productions which did have a general use and pass this on for what it may be worth. I had a set of flats, made from $2'' \times 1''$ frames, faced with hardboard. They are, of course, heavier than the more usual canvas-covered flats, but they are a good deal more durable and also look more solid and realistic in a small hall. But a box set made from such flats is a pretty static commodity and does not lend itself to rapid changes, so I devised one flat, the appearance of which could be altered very quickly

Fig. 7 Multi-purpose flat

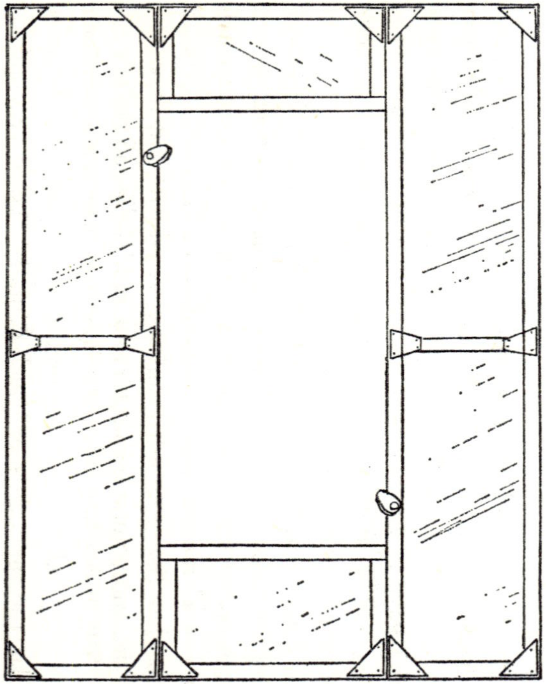

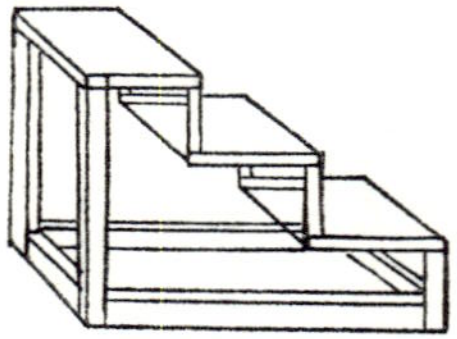

Stairs for Door

Back View of Flat

and easily. It was fundamentally the same as all the other flats, but had a centre section that could be removed, held in place behind by wooden buttons. We then made three more centre sections of the same dimensions, one of them including a hinged rectangular door, another a door with an arched top, and the third a casement window. In addition, we made a small set of steps rising to the height of the bottom edge of the centre aperture. This one flat could then have the appearance of a wall, two different kinds of door, or a window, and could be changed between scenes in a very short space of time. With this piece strategically placed at a focal point, changing it gave the illusion of a complete scene change.

Having worked for years on a stage that is only fifteen feet wide and twelve feet deep, with a solid ceiling seven feet six inches above the stage and, for much of the time, only one access point, down left, I think you will agree that there were problems enough. Yet we have always found ways of getting round these problems and have never allowed the physical limitations determine our choice of plays. I am quite sure that you should always let your material determine the set and never the other way round.

In my experience, the best way to approach the set design for any play is to discover first of all the problems that are going to be presented by the action, find a solution to these problems, and then evolve the rest of the set around those solutions. Perhaps I can best demonstrate this with one more illustration.

It has always been our policy to programme around Christmastime a play for children, and on one occasion we decided to present an adaptation of the Hans Andersen story, *The Snow Queen*. There are a great many scenes in this play, starting in Granny's garret, proceeding via 'the road to the north' and a robbers' camp to the great Ice Palace of the Snow Queen, and finally back again to the garret. The Queen and her Chancellor appear and disappear mysteriously, and, among other things, a rose bush is instantly withered by a magic spell. Needless to say, it is later required to be restored to bloom equally quickly. Now an audience of children always proves more enthusiastic than an audience of adults; they are much more ready to use their imaginations, and will accept a great deal at face value. But they love spectacles and magical effects and the very young ones need colourful visual elements to hold their attention when perhaps the dialogue gets a bit heavy-going. So, how to set about solving the problems of staging *The Snow Queen*?

The first gleam of hope stems from the fact that the play has a narrator, Mr. Storyteller, who sometimes talks directly to the audience and sometimes gets involved in the action himself. His presence on stage is therefore at all times acceptable to the audience, and as he 'unfolds' the development of the plot, it seems logical that he might also quite literally 'unfold' the scenery, and make the changes in full view, whilst talking. Problem number one, *how* to make scene changes, is on the way to being solved.

Next, we look for any aspect that can be common to all scenes: some feature that is pertinent to all the locations and can be a permanent part of the set. Well, the whole play takes place in

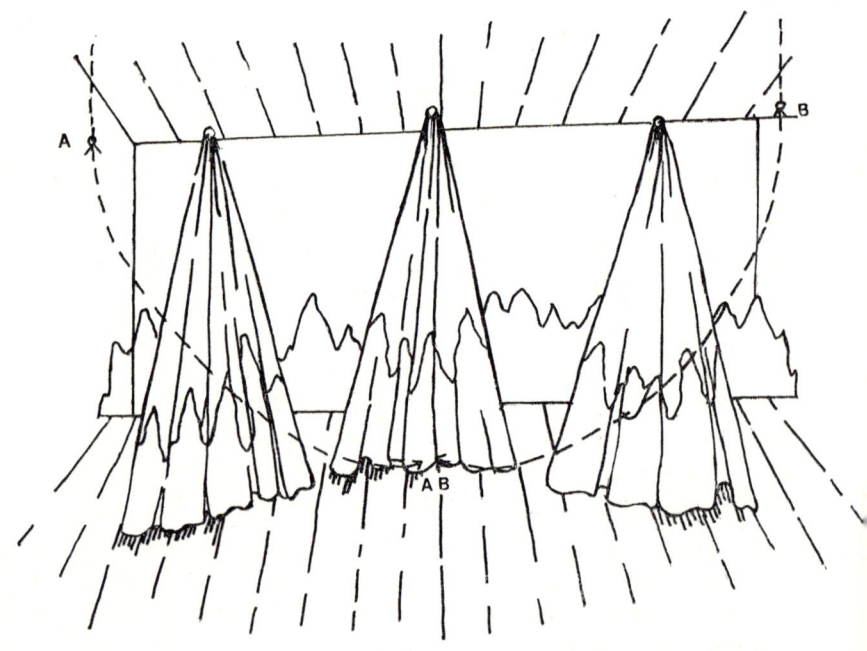

Fig. 8   The three mountains for 'The Snow Queen' set

winter, and we are constantly either hearing about or actually in 'the frozen north.' So, how about a row of glittering icy peaks, set along the cyclorama? They could be glimpsed through the window of Granny's garret, form the backing in all their splendour for the road to the north and the robbers' camp, and also be seen dimly through the icicles of the Queen's palace. That is our starting point, then: a ground row of mountain peaks, cut from hardboard, painted blue and white, with glitter glued on the points, and permanently set up-stage. But how is one man going to cope with setting up and striking three different interiors, quickly and easily? Perhaps if he could virtually gather each set in his arms and fold it up it might be the answer. Sheets? We could certainly paint interiors on pairs of sheets sewn together like book-flats and hung from the ceiling. Yes, Mr. Storyteller could easily fold those up at the end of each scene, but what is he

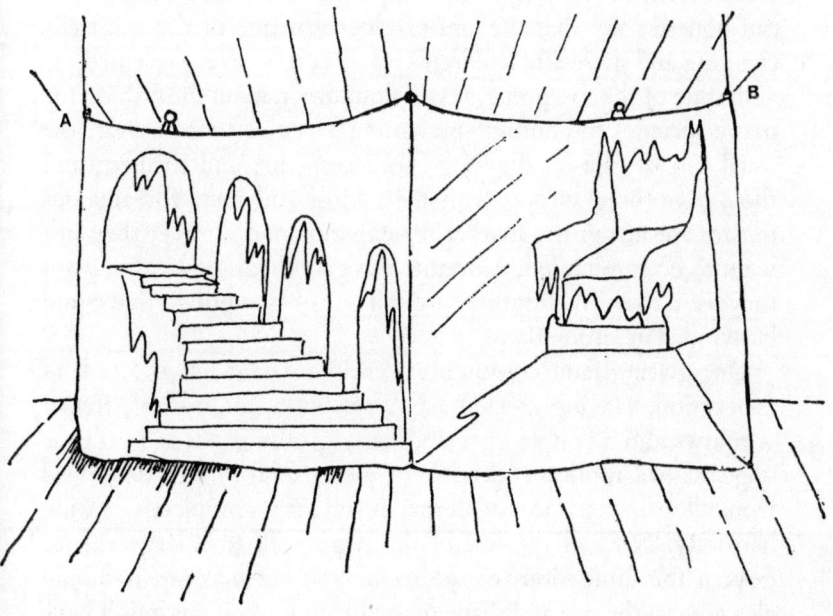

Fig. 9 One *mountain* opened to reveal Snow Queen's palace

to do then? Carry them on and off every time? Wait a minute, perhaps they could be left *on* stage, to look like something else!

With that kind of thought process, we finally arrived at the following solution. Three sets of sheets were assembled, and each one painted with a different scene on the inside. The garret set was suspended from a cup-hook stage-left, the robbers' tent from a hook stage-right, and the palace up-stage centre. Hanging only from the middle hooks, each set of sheets looked rather like a bell tent, and when sprayed on the outside with blue and glitter looked exactly like an icy mountain. Mr. Storyteller merely had to gather up the two loose corners hanging down onto the stage, open up the sheets and hook those corners onto the ceiling and we had the appropriate interior in seconds.

The Queen and Chancellor made their mysterious entrances and exits during brief black-outs, and the Storyteller took the same opportunity to turn round the cut-out, free-standing rose bush, painted on one side with full blooms, and on the other with faded roses. The cost of all this was, as you can see, minimal, but I can honestly say that the end-product was one of the most enchanting and successful children's plays we have ever presented.

In spite of the foregoing, it will doubtless remain the fashion for many societies to continue presenting, once or twice a year, the usual run of one-set drawing-room comedies and thrillers, and there is nothing wrong with that. Most audiences for amateur theatre are not in the market for experimental theatre; they just want to be entertained. All right, let's give them the kind of plays they seem to enjoy, but there are still one or two pitfalls that could be avoided in setting them.

One glaring fault commonly seen in amateur sets is a lack of proportion. Having erected a box set with, say, a door, french windows and a couple of walls, many groups proceed to fill the stage with a motley collection of pieces of furniture borrowed from all over the place, of all shapes and sizes, completely lacking harmony. Now as the size of the stage will, to a large extent, govern the dimensions of the room you are making, it should also govern the size and shape of the furniture you put in it. I have found it well worth while to assemble, over the years, a small set of furniture scaled to my tiny stage and tailor-made for the job. We have a couple of tables, some stools and two or three benches

1 The author and his wife in 'Rattle of a Simple Man' for which a totally realistic set was built.

2 Realism again. A World War I dug-out of authentic proportions for the play 'Journey's End'.

3 An open air rehearsal of 'The Young Elizabeth'. Actors begin to get the feel of costumes and set while both are still under construction.

4 'The Young Elizabeth': the same production in performance. The mechanics of this set are further illustrated in Fig. 6 on pages 50 and 51.

5 A scene from 'Alice in Wonderland': the Dodo's feathers, Alice's dress and the Mock Turtle's shell were all painted to give texture.

6 The two crows, Karl and Klara, with Gerda in 'The Snow Queen'. The sheets closed to represent mountains (as illustrated in Fig. 8) can be seen in the background.

7 'The Snow Queen' with one of the *mountains* opened to reveal Granny's Garret.

8 A scene from 'The Heiress': the 'brocade velvet' wallpaper was hand painted, using a stencil, to give texture when correctly lit.

9 Pamela Matthew as 'The Heiress'. Note the deliberate use of small chairs and tables, lending a more spacious effect to a tiny stage.

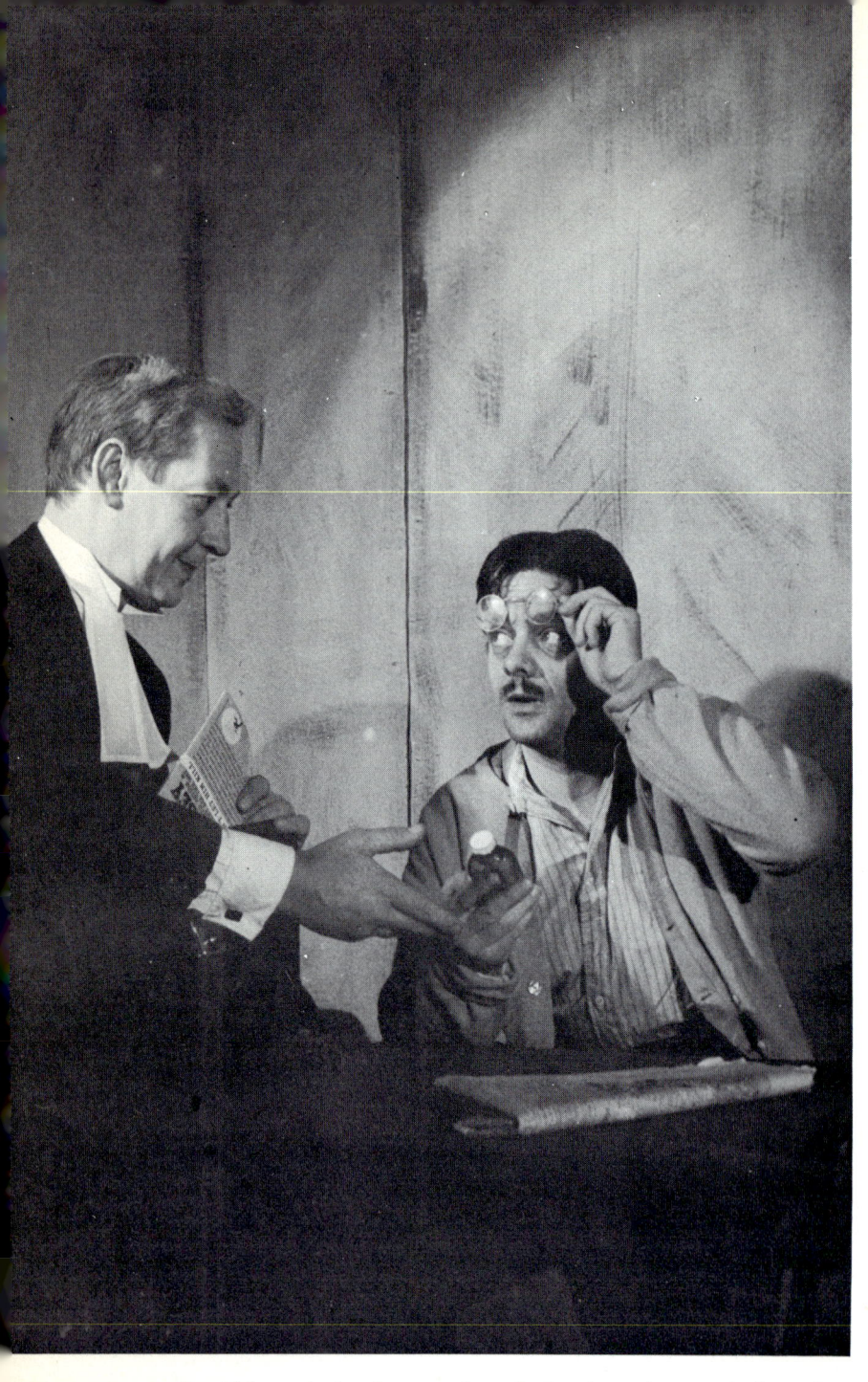

10 David Jason, before he turned professional, working with the author in a production of John Mortimer's one-act play 'Dock Brief'.

11 The dramatic effect of actors *not* facing each other illustrated by this duologue between Stanislas and the Queen in 'The Eagle has Two Heads'.

12 A scene from 'Who's Afraid of Virginia Woolf?' illustrating how the audience's attention can be focused on one player (in this case Martha on the left of the picture) by the grouping of the others.

13 Brian Matthew fulfils a long cherished ambition by playing the front legs of a pantomime horse.

which would be lost in a large living room, but look perfectly right in fifteen feet by twelve. I do, admittedly, have the help of an excellent carpenter, but in this age of do-it-yourself such assistance should not be hard to find. For a school group, the construction of scenery might prove an excellent practical exercise for the woodwork classes.

In the opening chapter of this book, when discussing the essential posts to be filled when forming a dramatic society, I was so carried away with the desirability of having a designer on the team that I forgot to mention that invaluable lady the Wardrobe Mistress. This is someone whose services will be in constant demand, whether the play in production is in costume or modern dress, so we really ought to take a look at the extent of her duties.

Basically, the Wardrobe Mistress is responsible for making sure that every member of the cast is equipped with everything that he or she has to wear during the play, that they make their first entrance looking the way the producer and/or designer intended them to look, and that they continue to make their entrances like that for the entire run. After the final curtain, she then has the job of ensuring that all clothes worn during the play are cleaned, repaired, stored, or returned whence they came.

Our ideal lady for the job must obviously be a super needle-woman. She will either have to make, or supervise the making of, a lot of costumes in a short space of time, or at the very least carry out emergency running repairs. Wherever she is stationed back-stage during a performance, her tools of trade should always be ready to hand, and these should include some perhaps less obvious items, such as stain removers. Let this paragon be warned that sartorial disaster strikes more frequently and more severely on stage than in everyday life. Buttons pop off in all directions, zips break, hooks gouge out their own eyes, trousers split, and sleeves, male and female, seem hell-bent on parting company with the main body of their garment. The perfect WM will always have a secret cache of assorted materials, cuff-links, collar studs, belt buckles, pieces of elastic and safety pins. She had better be a veritable walking haberdashery, and it will be a rare performance during which her resources are not tested.

If it is decided to hire costumes for a period production, the Wardrobe Mistress will obviously be very much involved throughout the entire operation. You will find that all the major costume firms print their own order forms with appropriate spaces for name of actor, name of character, height, waist measurement, inside leg, and so on. Some of these are so elaborate, requiring such refinements as 'distance from centre of back to wrist with arm bent', that you might think the dear fellows planned to tailor-make a whole set of costumes exclusively for two performances in your village hall! Just a word of warning to the unduly optimistic: when your costumes arrive you will be lucky if many of them fit the actors to any great extent. You will possibly wonder, as I have done on many an occasion, just why such detailed measurements were asked if they were to be totally disregarded. The truth of the matter is, of course, that most sets of costumes were originally made for professional productions and they eke out the remainder of their existence being adapted to fit amateurs of a variety of shapes and sizes. Though costumiers will hardly expect their customers to undertake major surgery on the articles they hire, they nevertheless accept as a fact of life the need for sundry Wardrobe Mistresses to make minor adjustments and running repairs.

When costumes are hired there is seldom any need to have them cleaned before returning them, as the cost of this is usually incorporated in the hire charge, but it is a point worth checking in the first place. If you are using your own wardrobe, on the other hand, costumes should always be cleaned immediately after use and before storing. Although they may only have been worn for a few hours, they are likely to have acquired make-up stains and furthermore they very soon begin to smell.

The really keen WM will always be on the look-out for bits and pieces that may come in useful at some future date and, provided she has space to house them, will never spurn offers of such items as dress suits and jodhpurs, for example. If she does build up a collection of costumes, she will probably not need reminding by me that it is essential to check at regular intervals for any possible traces of damage from moths or damp. I have known instances of garments taken from store at the eleventh hour riddled with holes in the most undisguisable areas.

Another feature that is frequently overlooked in both sets and costumes is their age. Not their period, but their age. Very few plays have been written for a cast of fashion models living in a show house! It may seem like over-stating the obvious, but it needs to be emphasised that 'well-dressed' doesn't necessarily mean dressed in new clothes, and 'well furnished' doesn't mean newly-furnished. Never be afraid to 'dirty down' costumes, so that they have a well-worn look and the actors can have an air of familiarity with their clothes. Fight your leading lady's inclination to have a hair-do for opening night, for it may be quite inappropriate to the part she is playing, and resist well-meant suggestions for decorating a set with beautiful ornaments quite out of place in the play you are presenting.

In the final analysis, it all comes back to the two characteristics I mentioned at the beginning of this chapter; uniformity of style, and texture. Keep those qualities firmly in mind, consider the individual needs and problems of every play you do, use your imagination to the full, and you will wind up with productions that not only sound good, but look good as well.

Chapter 7

Make-up

There seems to be a growing tendency among actors, including some professionals, to believe that, except for heavy character roles, make-up is unnecessary. It probably stems from the school of ultra-realism in the theatre in which any form of artificiality is decried. Yet what a strangely illogical premise this is: the very essence of theatre is the creation of the *illusion* of reality through artificial means. Otherwise we should surely build our sets with bricks and mortar and, to carry things to the absurd extreme, shoot the villain not with blanks but with real bullets. An actor is not a chameleon. He may *feel* florid or pale, fat or thin, entirely to his own satisfaction, but unless he is seen to be any of those things it will be very difficult to convince an audience of the fact. In any event, producers should never allow actors to decide for themselves whether or not make-up is necessary, for they are in the worst position to decide.

While it will be immediately obvious that an actor of thirty will need considerable disguise to appear eighty, it may not be so readily apparent that he also needs make-up to look his own age, naturally, on stage. He needs make-up for two reasons.

First, even in a small auditorium, quite modestly-powered spot lights tend to wash out natural facial colour, and in a large hall it is necessary to amplify features, to project them to someone sitting quite a long way from the stage. You can convince yourself of the effect of lighting on your face by observing what it does to scenery. Take a look at the colours on a set under a low-powered working light and then notice how those colours change quite palpably under the greater wattage of spots shone through gelatines. Basically, the tone of a gelatine will cancel out similar shades in anything it illuminates, so you will see that, for instance, pinks or more intense shades will eliminate the natural colours of the face, giving a very pale, white effect. Therefore, when the colour of the face is heightened by the use of make-up, that in turn is rendered down by the lighting, and the end result is, or should be, a natural appearance.

Second, persuade a colleague, without make-up, to stand on stage under full lighting while you take a seat at the back of the auditorium. You will almost certainly discover that features are not at all sharply delineated. The whites of the eyes will blend with the surrounding skin, and seriously diminish the power of expression. The mouth and nose may also lack the definition that they had at a range of three feet. So, just as we found we had to add texture to sets and costumes to give the illusion of reality, we also need to give texture to the face for the same reason. We not only have to heighten colour to achieve a natural effect, we also have to paint in shadows and high-lights to give shape and form.

The art of make-up is a fascinating aspect of the actor's craft, and, like acting itself, one that can really only be learned in practice. Books and diagrams can be of some help initially, and experts can certainly offer guidance and advice, but the best teacher is, as in most things, experience. It never ceases to amaze me that some amateurs seem to be content to allow the producer or a back-stage worker to apply their make-up for them when, with practice and patience, they could gain the great satisfaction of learning to do it themselves. I have always found the hour before curtain-up the most valuable time for getting into character, and as I see my appearance in the mirror changing under my own hands I really begin to feel myself the character I am about to portray. For this reason above all others I strongly urge any newcomer to acting to acquire his own make-up and to spend time in learning how to use it.

If we consider first the essential basic ingredients of a make-up box, perhaps we can then go on to discussing how to use them. The wide variety of grease-paint colours available will amaze and confuse the beginner. When I was a student, the whole range could be purchased for a fairly modest outlay, and the wealthier ones among us would also buy elaborate metal boxes with cantilevered trays, mirrors and lights that popped up like a mighty Wurlitzer! Such extravagant excesses are, luckily, quite unnecessary, for the price of make-up has risen so exorbitantly that such an elaborate set would cost a small fortune. Furthermore, you would almost certainly find that even after several years half the sticks of paint would remain untouched in their cellophane wrappers. Many of them are for special effects that are seldom needed and are therefore best obtained only if and when required. In any case, you are going to find that starting even a modest make-up kit from scratch will cost several pounds, though the good news is that it should last for a very long time.

The most commonly used grease-paints are those manufactured by Leichner and they are fairly readily obtainable. They come in three thicknesses but are pretty uniform in length. The base, or foundation colours are the fattest, then the various shades of carmine are somewhat thinner, and the slenderest of all are the liners; brown, black, blue, grey and purple or lake. The base colours are known by numbers from one to twenty, and just to complicate matters some of these are further sub-divided into half-numbers. But don't despair, you are not going to need anything like all of these. Requirements for men and women will vary slightly, but for the most part they are common to both. First you will need a number $2\frac{1}{2}$ which is pink in colour, and principally most useful to women. Then a 5, a light yellowish colour; a 6, which is the nearest to a natural average flesh tint; an 8, which is reddish-brown; a 9; which is similar but deeper brown; a 16, a dark brown, almost black, and a 20, which is white. I would add to these a couple of sticks known by names, rather than numbers, and they are Chrome, a rather deep bright yellow, and Green. You could safely leave those two out if you are counting the pennies. I have had the same two sticks in my box for about twenty years, but they do come in useful from time to time.

The slightly thinner carmine sticks are numbered Carmine I, II and III, and you should find that the bright I and much darker III will meet all eventualities. Next we come to the thin liners, and I should recommend a Spotlite brown, Lake liner, light and dark blue, light and dark grey, and a black.

In addition to the foregoing you will also need powder, which again comes in several shades, but the most generally useful is probably the one known as Rose Blending, though I might add that I have, when pushed by poverty, successfully used a much cheaper talcum or baby powder. Similarly, Leichner make an excellent grease-paint removal cream, but make-up can also be taken off satisfactorily with olive oil, liquid paraffin or even lard. I've used them all at one time or another, but if you can afford it, it is much pleasanter to use the proper removal cream.

I'm afraid this is turning into a long list, but we haven't quite finished yet. Checking over the contents of my own box, I find that I also have a small bottle of black tooth enamel, for blacking out teeth; several plastic bottles of blow-on grey powder for the hair (becoming less necessary as the years go by!), and some liquid white, also for hair. Then I have numerous hanks of different coloured crepe hair, for beards and moustaches; a bottle of spirit gum for sticking them on, and also tubes of artifix, a rather evil-smelling paste for the same purpose.

In general, when applying grease-paint, you should use one hand as a palette and the fingers of the other as brushes, but it is also useful to have a couple of thin, fine-haired paint brushes; a bundle of orange sticks; a few hair-grips (even for men); a roll of cotton wool and a box of tissues. Some people also include a soft baby-brush for removing excess powder from the face. Nice, but inessential. As to a container for this lot, I have always housed my grease-paints in a couple of medium-sized cigar boxes, subdivided with strips of cardboard. All the other items go into a separate, somewhat larger box.

Now we have our make-up kit ready let us, in theory, put it to use. In the early stages, you should always try to practise under ideal conditions. Later on you may have to cope with inadequate surroundings, but then you will be able to fall back on memory and knowledge of how certain effects are obtained. In the beginning you must be able to see quite clearly what you are doing. More important, you must be able to see by artificial light. Working in daylight is extremely difficult because it will not render down the colour you are applying and its diffused nature will neither cast shadows in the right places nor pick out the painted highlights that you will apply. Similarly, a single overhead light will be equally inefficient for the reasons discussed in the chapter on stage-lighting. Ideally, you should sit facing a large mirror which has several 100-watt bulbs placed around it at short intervals, along the top and down both sides.

Let us assume that you wish to put on what is called a 'straight' make-up: in other words, you want to appear on stage naturally as yourself. Now despite the fact that I have described certain colours as base or foundation colours, any single one of these is seldom sufficient on its own and it is necessary to blend them exactly as a painter will blend his raw colours on a palette. For a start, try mixing your number 5 and number 9 by rubbing a quantity of each into the palm of one hand and then blending them together until you have the tone you want. Then, with the finger tips of the other hand, smear the mixture evenly all over your face, taking great care to carry it up and into the hairline, under the chin onto the neck, and behind the neck. Do this as evenly as you are able, and then use a tissue to blot all the areas you have covered, removing any excess patches of grease. Next, concentrate on the eyes. In order to give them definition, as I mentioned earlier, take an orange stick and cover the point with a dark brown (Spotlite or 16, which are the same colour) or a black liner, and then draw a fine line along the lower lid, just below the lashes, extending just beyond the natural corner of the eye. Women will then probably add either a light blue or grey liner colour to the whole of the upper lid, but this is not necessary for men. The mouth, too, needs tinting, using grease paint exactly like a lip-stick. While women will choose to use carmine, this does *look* like lipstick, and a more natural effect is achieved for a man by using a number 8. For a large theatre it is quite a good idea to take this a stage further and to use one of the small brushes to etch a very fine darker line (lake liner against carmine; number 9 against number 8) around the outline of the mouth. For a young, healthy complexion, add a touch of carmine to the top of the cheeks, but use this very sparingly and blend it into the base carefully, or you will look like a wooden soldier with red spots on his cheeks. To thin down somewhat plump features, mix a shadow of number 16 and lake and smear this delicately into the place where the hollows of the cheek should be. But – and this is most important – remember that no shadow will look like a shadow without its accompanying highlight, so above the shaded area, along the cheek bone, paint a strip of number 5, also taking care to blend the edges of this into the colour underneath.

When you have completed the painting to your satisfaction, again use tissues to blot the face and then powder all over with blending powder. This has two effects: it will decrease the intensity of the colour you have applied, which is why it is known as 'powdering down' and you must allow for this when putting colour on in the first place, and secondly it sets the make-up, acting as a sort of fixative, which prevents it running and smudging when you are under the lights. Do make certain when you have finished that you dust off any visible powder, either with a puff, cotton wool, or a soft brush. One further tip which I have found helps somewhat, particularly in very hot weather, is after completing the make-up and powdering to immerse the whole of the face in a basin of cold water. This will not prevent but it will reduce perspiration.

The procedure for any make-up is fundamentally the same, though of course if you wish to change your features or to increase your age the details will be more elaborate. One important difference to remember if you are going to wear a wig is that the wig should be put on first. This does not apply to women's wigs, generally, but to those for men which have, say, a bald pate and high forehead. The base colour is then applied to the face and the wig base, ensuring an even all-over colour. Wigs always used to be made on close-fitting canvas caps and it was extraordinarily difficult to get the same colour on canvas as on skin, and even more difficult to disguise the wig join. Recently, however, largely thanks to the requirements of television, a form of plastic cap or wig base has been developed. It is almost a natural colour to start with, and is fixed in place with a liquid plastic sealant painted along the join. This forms an artificial 'skin' between the wig line and the natural skin and is scarcely detectable to the naked eye at close range. It also takes grease-paint much more easily. I recently gave a performance in a private house, playing an old, completely bald man, and used one of these wigs. The audience, incidentally, was practically sitting in my lap. After the performance, the wig removed, they refused to believe that I had in fact played the part, which surely speaks volumes for the efficacy of this new development.

The preparation of moustaches and beards is a long and tedious job and I'm afraid that nowadays, out of sheer laziness, I usually have them specially made. When done like this, the hair is attached to a light, scarcely visible gauze and is very easy to fix in place with spirit gum. It is equally easy to remove, and remains intact for the next performance. However, this is rather expensive and not really justified against a production budget unless you are going to give a great many performances. The cheaper alternative is to make your own, using crepe hair. This comes in tightly plaited hanks in a great range of colours, but cannot be used in the form in which you buy it. When the hank is untied, it will be found to open out into crimped lengths, and all too often I have seen amateurs who have merely cut off a piece and stuck it straight onto their face, resulting in a remarkably curly and completely false-looking moustache or beard. The correct procedure is to untie the hair, soak it overnight in cold water, then hang it up to dry with a weight suspended on the end to take out the curls. It can then be cut into short lengths and a beard built up gradually on the face, starting underneath the chin line and then adding further pieces on the front of the face, so that the two together give a realistic thickness of hair. Before attaching either beard or moustache, it is necessary to wipe away all grease-paint from the areas to be covered, as spirit gum will not set properly on top of grease paint, and your hairy appendages are quite liable to drop off during performance! I have occasionally experimented with the construction of a more permanent sort of beard by first sticking pieces of thin bandage onto the chin and then adding the crepe hair to the bandage. It was then possible to remove the whole beard at one go, shortening the time needed to apply it on subsequent performances. I have never been entirely happy with results obtained in this way, but it might be worth trying. Before leaving the subject of false hair, there is one more point worth mentioning. If you take careful note of all the men you see with natural beards you will find that in many cases the shade of the beard is different from the shade of the hair. A fair-haired man will often be seen to have a ginger beard; medium-hair sometimes goes with a darker chin growth, while it is very common for the beard to turn grey, or even white, long before the hair on the head. For total realism, one should perhaps follow suit when putting on a false beard, and yet it always seems to me to increase the appearance of artificiality. Perhaps this is one area in which we should not quite 'hold the mirror up to nature.'

Now let us take a look at the way to go about make-up for an old character, since this is very often required and frequently seems to lead inexperienced players into total disaster. Time and again one sees a young actor who has applied a straight make-up and then criss-crossed his face with a veritable network of thin lines drawn in lake liner, so that he looks more like a full colour map of the London Underground than an elderly person. I have never discovered quite how this universal misconception arose, but is it due, I wonder, to the common but inaccurate description of a 'lined' face? Those lines are really shadows falling in wrinkles, or creases of the skin caused by the slackening of the facial flesh which comes with age, and there is the clue to the way in which we can simulate age: not by drawing lines, but by painting shadows. and, as I stressed earlier, the highlights that go with those shadows.

First, though, we should consider the base colour for an old face and this of course will be determined by the character. A vigorous open-air type such as a farmer, or sailor, will have that weather-beaten, almost tanned leather appearance, but an old man who has spent much of his life indoors, possibly in artificial light, will be basically much lighter, even almost grey in appearance. A good base for this is the number 6, unmixed with any other colour, for although it looks like flesh colour in daylight (it is in fact sometimes used as a cosmetic to conceal a facial scar), it assumes a much more pallid look under lights.

Next, let us think of what has happened to a face with the advance of years. In all probability the cheeks will have hollowed and the flesh will droop in folds from the side of the nostrils to the corners of the mouth, thus giving greater prominence to the cheek bones. The temples tend to sink in as well, emphasising the top of the forehead, while wrinkles on the brow are much more noticeable. Then the nose will often be less fleshy, giving sharper focus to the bone at the bridge. The eyes recede deeper into their sockets, increasing the folds of skin under the lower lid. The jaw line sags, the mouth is drawn tighter, and the neck assumes a scrawny appearance.

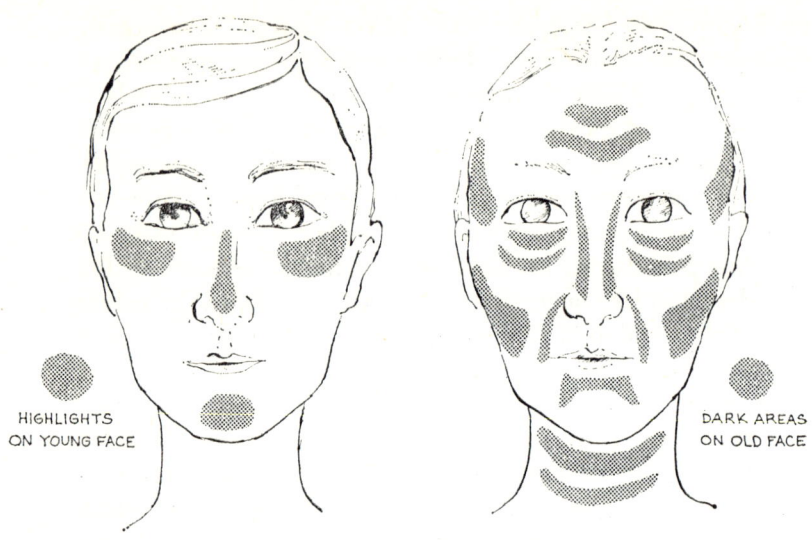

Fig. 10 Make-up

The most important thing to remember when setting out to create the sort of face I have just described by means of make-up is that the best result will come from a broad, bold method. Heavy shadows and pronounced highlights always look more effective than thinly-drawn lines. This may be hard to believe at first, but I assure you it is true and there is a way in which you can prove it for yourself. The best way to assess your own make-up as it will appear to an audience is to look at it in the mirror through half-closed eyes because you are only three feet away from your own image, while they will be anything from ten to a hundred or more. Now, regarding your efforts in this way, thinly-drawn lines will virtually disappear, but bold shadows and highlights will look like the wrinkles they are meant to suggest.

If you are to play a part several times it is best to evolve a routine of make-up and this will vary with individual actors. Personally, after applying a base, I always begin with the eyes. Using one of the small paint brushes, I first apply a mixture of 16 and lake to the inner corner of the upper lid, extending to the side of the bridge of the nose and up to the eyebrow. Then, with brush or finger-tip, I paint a fairly broad band of shadow in an arc under the eye. Next, the sides of the nose are shaded, and broad shadows added from the corner of the nostrils, round the bottom of the cheek, and downwards from the corners of the mouth. I then apply patches of shadow to the cheeks, below the cheek bones; to the temples, and on the naturally sunken areas of the neck. By furrowing the brow, I note carefully where the wrinkles are, and shade these areas broadly, in broken lines, adding one or perhaps two vertical creases between the eyebrows. Incidentally, a broad shadow is another useful way of disguising a wig join on the forehead. Next, using a number 5 grease paint, I add highlights to all the areas I have just shaded, including the brow, cheek bones, bridge of the nose and on the neck.

Thinning and tightening the mouth I always find a difficult job. The base colour will initially have been applied all over the lips, and you can now paint, with say a number 8, a lip that is inside your own natural line, and it is a good idea then to add tiny touches of 16, or your 16 and lake shadow mixture, all around the line of the mouth. A further useful idea, if you want to give the appearance of old, rheumy eyes, is to paint, with a brush, carmine onto the inside of the lower lid, above the lashes. This is a slightly painful procedure and will probably make your eyes water, but this soon wears off and the effect is tremendous.

If you want to change the colour of your own hair, the stage of make-up at which you do this will probably depend on the method you are using. For example, my hair is medium brown in colour, and a producer once wanted me to have raven-black hair. She suggested rubbing it all over with sheets of carbon paper, and this really does work beautifully. It is a messy procedure and should obviously be done first of all, and it does mean that you will need to wash your hair after every performance. Similarly, a good way of whitening the hair is to apply wet blanco with a small sponge, or wet white from a bottle. After it has dried, comb and brush your hair, to prevent it from matting and lying flat to the head. Again, this is something you need to do first. If, on the other hand, you are going to blow dry white or grey powder onto your hair, this can safely be done after you have completed the rest of your make-up.

Finally, particularly with a heavy character make-up, do not forget your hands. The most brilliant and skilfully applied facial aging will be spoiled if you are seen to have the hands of a vigorous youngster. You should use the same technique, shading the sides of the fingers and highlighting the tops, adding lateral shading on the knuckles. Obviously, this must be the last stage of all, when you have no need to touch your face make-up again. Incidentally, it should seldom be necessary to repair the ravages during a performance, but it is wise to keep powder and puff handy as you will often need to 'dry off' your make-up when you come off stage and during intervals, otherwise it is apt to smudge.

If this chapter has inspired any newcomers to the stage to learn to do their own make-up that is splendid, but I should like to add one more general piece of advice. Always allow yourself plenty of time. I have known ill-mannered and inconsiderate actors who rush into the dressing-room only minutes before curtain up, hastily slap on make-up, and get on stage. On the other hand, even now I sometimes get part of the way through my routine, decide I don't like the result, clean it all off and start again, but if I had not allowed plenty of time in the first place I should certainly start to panic and my performance would undoubtedly suffer. You can also learn quite a lot about make-up by studying original portraits, because the technique of oil-painting has a lot in common with the application of grease-paint, particularly in the use of shadows and highlights. This is much more helpful than trying to analyse the methods of professionals in the theatre, because if they have done their job well, you will not be able to see *how* they have done it.

Chapter 8

Getting It All Together

So far in this book we have considered principally the skills and crafts required by the various individuals who make up a dramatic society: the producer, stage-manager, actor, lighting technician, designer and wardrobe mistress. But none of these can practise his hobby alone. Amateur theatre is, or should be, one of the most closely integrated of group activities. And yet it is precisely when considered *as* a group that many societies appear to fall down, mainly because they stagger along from production to production with no over-all planning. So in this chapter I shall devote a little time to those often neglected areas, arranging a season and working out a schedule for a single production from first reading to first night.

For a considerable period I was associated with a Little Theatre group, as an actor and occasionally as a producer, which to everyone's astonishment managed for eight months of every year to present a play a month, running each production for ten nights. Yet seldom, if ever, during the run of one play did anyone know what the next one was going to be, who was going to produce it, or who was going to appear in it. The result was inevitably an ill-balanced hotch-potch of a programme, under-rehearsed productions, hastily-built and tatty sets, and a nagging, demoralising sense of lack of direction for all concerned. If the unbelievable amount of time wasted had been put to use, that theatre might have been flourishing today, which it isn't!

At the other end of the scale there are numerous societies who are content to present one, or perhaps two productions a year, each one running for a couple of nights. These are really societies in name only, with one or two regular stalwarts who more or less keep things going, and an otherwise changing personnel because there is insufficient activity to sustain interest.

Since it is my declared purpose to offer guide-lines mainly for absolute beginners in this book, let us think about a possible programme for a new group. The number of productions that can be presented in any one season, or year, will obviously be determined to some extent by the nature of the community in and for which you perform. If you live in a very small town or village it may seem to you impossible to cajole a hall-full of local inhabitants to support you more than twice in a twelve-month, while the activities of a school group may on the one hand be limited to term-time and on the other restricted by dreaded examinations. However, I do think that one should aim at a minimum of four different presentations a year. Many years ago, I was invited to take over production for a village group, long established, but at the time in question defunct. They had been doing two plays a year, and performing each one for two nights. I immediately increased the programme to four, and the run of each to three performances, and to their utter amazement the audience grew so much that before long the number of performances had to be increased still further and even matinees were added. You see, once you have a captive audience and provided they are sufficiently impressed by the standard of your performance, if you can announce in your programme that the next production in three months time will be such and such a play you create a continuity of interest and you might even receive some bookings that far in advance. If you announce nothing, and start production again six or more months later, you will have to start finding an audience all over again. Furthermore, with productions closer together you can afford to offer a much wider range of plays and that is something that works to everyone's advantage, players and playgoers alike.

So, we have settled on a projected programme of four productions over a period of a year. Next we should decide on four different categories, and I found an eminently workable formula to be: a light comedy, farce or classical comedy in the Spring; an open-air Shakespeare or costume classic in the summer; a modern drama or serious play in the autumn, and a seasonal play around Christmas. This routine was adhered to fairly closely by that village society I mentioned for close on ten years, and during that time we also added pantomimes, presented just after Christmas.

It is essential, I firmly believe, for the producer and his production team to select all the plays to be performed a year in advance, so that not only can a full programme be announced to the public, which shows you really mean business, but a lot of the preparatory work can be put in hand, thereby conserving precious rehearsal time later on. If you are lucky enough to have more than one producer they will be able to start doing their homework with plenty of time to spare. It may also be possible to evolve sets, or pieces of scenery, which with very little adaptation can be utilised in all four productions. If costumes are to be hired, they can be reserved well ahead of schedule, and if they are to be made then the makers will appreciate plenty of warning. It also seems to be the trend these days for some of the better amateur actors to owe no allegiance to any particular group, but to flit from one to another, by invitation. If you need to augment your group with such players, and I frequently find that I have to do so, you will find that they have to be 'booked' almost like professionals, so once again forward planning comes into its own. In fact, having chosen all your plays, it is a good idea to cast them as far as possible, though this is one thing that will have to remain a little flexible. Unheralded bouts of 'flu, or unforeseen professional commitments, for example, are bound to make changes necessary somewhere along the line.

Production budgets should also be worked out in detail for a whole season in advance, so that producers will have guidance as to whether they can afford to be elaborate or whether simplicity is the order of the day. It is a regrettable fact that most artistically creative people are pretty hopeless when it comes to finance, so if you can persuade some hard-headed accountant to join your committee as treasurer you should do so. Production costs can be estimated fairly accurately, because you will know, for instance, how much you are going to have to pay in royalties, the cost of hiring costumes, furniture or properties, rental for the hall, including extras for lighting and heating, and the price of printing tickets, programmes and posters, or of placing advertisements in the local paper. What you cannot know with any accuracy in advance is the income from your productions, and it may be disastrous to count on full houses for all performances. Work on a basis of say sixty to seventy per cent capacity, and then prune the expenditure budget to fall somewhere below that figure and you should be fairly safe. Sell-out productions will then provide a useful little bonus which can be earmarked for adding to your stock of lighting equipment, for example, or on other items that will be permanent assets.

Having considered the planning of a whole season, let us turn now to the planning of an individual production. Haphazard rehearsal methods are all too common in the world of amateur theatre and lead to some very poor, ill-balanced productions, weak in some scenes and quite strong in others. The run-up to a first night needs to be accurately paced so that the cast come to the mark relaxed and full of confidence, not tired out, ill-tempered and tetchy with each other. If everything has been properly gauged, the dress rehearsal should run like a first performance without an audience. Those that drag on through a nightmare of chaos into the small hours of the morning must inevitably shatter confidence and result in an off-peak first night.

One is frequently asked how long a play should be rehearsed and although the answer will vary from producer to producer and will depend to some extent on the play concerned, I have always found the best results come from concentrated work over a relatively short period. (Yes, I *do* know that Stanislavsky spent three years on rehearsing *Hamlet* with the Moscow Arts Theatre!). In my opinion, three rehearsals a week for about three weeks and then every day for a final week are far more effective than one a week for six months. Ideas can develop and progress satisfactorily without wasting time on re-capping what was done at the previous session. Interest is sustained and actors don't get bored.

I find I usually need to spend the first three rehearsals setting the play. That is to say, walking the cast through all the moves which I have previously worked out. This is also the time for the producer to make quite sure that the stage-manager and all the actors take careful note of all such moves in their books, because this will prevent a lot of arguments later on.

This seems a suitable point to explain for beginners the basic

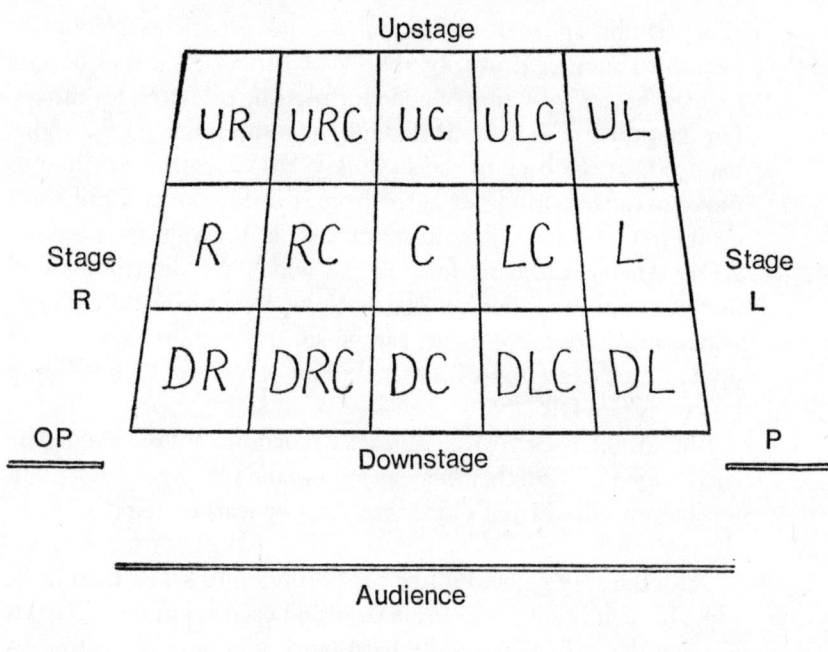

Fig. 11 Stage positions

language of play-setting and the abbreviations commonly used for this purpose. The first thing to remember is that all directions are given from the viewpoint of the actor, *facing* the auditorium, so that when he is told to exit stage-left he will go off to *his* left although to anyone sitting in the audience he will have gone off to the right. As you will see at once this could lead to confusion between producer working facing the stage and actor working facing the auditorium unless we had that basic agreement. So, let me repeat, all directions are given from the actor's angle, facing front. Next, the stage is divided into three strips, running across from left to right. Each of these strips is then further divided into five sections, so that we have a stage area divided into fifteen parts, as shown in Fig. 11. Since each part is named and has its own abbreviation, and that instructions to move or 'cross' from one section to another is usually abbreviated to an X, it will be seen that we have a very simple code for plotting all necessary moves. For example, if an actor is standing at some point on the right-hand side at the back of the stage (say UR) and we want him to move to the left-hand side at the front, the director will call 'cross down left' and he will write in his text at the appropriate point XDL. That is the basic formula by which the directions of all moves are plotted. Further elaborations, for example the *way* in which such moves are made, can be left to the individual and are perhaps best expressed with the addition of a word, such as 'Limp LC' or 'Stride DR'.

But to get back to our rehearsal schedule. Actors should be encouraged to learn their lines as soon as the play has been set, but not before. Moves and words can then be learned together as an entity.

With the play set, and the actors beginning to know their lines, I like to spend two or three rehearsals on each act in turn, for this is when the bulk of the really hard work is done and most progress made with character development, interpretation, and pace. At the end of the week devoted to the second act, it is useful to spend one rehearsal revising the first and if possible another one putting first and second acts together.

When the final week is reached, a complete run-through of the play should be attempted, even if it turns out to be more of a 'stagger through'. This is almost certain to reveal some sections of the play that are weaker than others and you still have time in hand to concentrate a couple of rehearsal sessions to those sections, but try to arrange things so that you have at least two or three more full runs before you come to the final dress rehearsal. At these full length sessions, the producer must resist the temptation to stop the action repeatedly to polish small points. His actors are gaining much more by being allowed to feel the flow of the play as a whole. The best procedure is to take notes during the rehearsal, and to give these notes at the end of each act, while the details are still fresh in mind. At all these full rehearsals, the cast should have all the props they will be using in the play, costumes or substitutes must be worn, and incidentals such as sound effects should be included. In this way actors grow gradually accustomed to the trappings of a production, and nothing is left to surprise them on the first public performance.

As a producer, I always try to fit in one additional rehearsal that does not involve the cast. A technical rehearsal. This is for the benefit of lighting and stage-management, and we run through the mechanics of the play without any dialogue, checking all cues and lighting changes, sound effects, music, and scene changes. Those responsible for all these ingredients need to be as relaxed and confident as the actors, and it helps them get into the right frame of mind if they can have just one 'dress rehearsal' of their own. They will also appreciate the presence of a couple of volunteers, whether members of the cast or not is unimportant, prepared to stand on stage or move about as instructed as a check on the effect of lights and the fall of shadows.

I have said before, but it is worth emphasising, that rehearsals are most beneficial if they can be conducted on the stage where performances are to take place, but if this is impossible – and regrettably it often is – then do make every effort to rehearse in a space of the same dimensions. And do try to use furniture of the right proportions as well. It is incredibly disconcerting to have to cope in performance with a chair twice as big as one that has been used in rehearsal.

Finally, having worked out a rehearsal schedule to your own satisfaction, make every effort to stipulate exactly what is to be covered at each session and bend over backwards to stick to that plan. You will find that many actors for some strange reason like to keep going over the bits they know best and are quite lazy about tackling the scenes that present problems. It gives them a false sense of security. And never, never tolerate that hoary old remark, 'It will be all right on the night', for believe me, without careful and complete preparation it most certainly will not be.

Chapter 9

Sound Effects

As one who has spent the greater part of his working life in radio, I have always been fascinated by the study of sound effects. In a play, a well chosen and strategically-placed sound can strike deep memory chords in an audience and sometimes set a scene more vividly than a visible set and much more quickly than a spoken description. Again, sound can extend the range of action in an audience's imagination by conjuring up pictures of the scene off-stage and out of sight. Life is not lived in a vacuum, nor in a sound-proof booth, so plays should not give the impression that it is. The illusion of reality can often be enhanced by the incidental use of effects not always specified by the author. Some sounds are, of course, called for in the text and are mentioned in the dialogue so that they become cues themselves and their absence would impede the action.

Unfortunately, this highly important aspect of production is not always accorded due consideration even in the professional theatre and the illusion created by the most realistic sets and impressive acting can be let down by badly reproduced sound. How much more important, then, should good sound be to amateur productions in which we have to attempt to create our illusions in less sophisticated surroundings and sometimes, let it be admitted, with less skilful players.

In the early days of theatre, all sound effects had to be produced 'live', by stage-managers and extras with the aid of a few simple mechanical devices such as wind machines and thunder sheets. Then came the advance of the panotrope, which was usually a desk with one or two turntables from which 78 r.p.m. records were played into a loud-speaker. This was certainly an improvement in some respects, but introduced the difficulty of finding the appropriate spot on a swiftly rotating record, the added hazards of scratches and recurring grooves, and the unfortunate aspect that all sounds emanated from one apparent source whatever the actual physical source was supposed to be. This could often lead to unwanted laughter in serious scenes. For example, imagine the ludicrous situation of an actor looking out of a window, right, referring to the arrival of a cab, and the audience hearing that cab quite plainly, apparently driving through the prompt corner down left.

With the enormous technical advances in Hi-Fi equipment in recent years it is now possible to record effects with an uncanny degree of realism, to reproduce them with the utmost fidelity, and to place the sound pretty well exactly where we want it.

In my own small theatre I have had installed a console which includes two stereo tape-recorders, one cassette player and two turntables. There is a mixer through which we can feed the sound from any individual one of those sources, or a combination of any four of the five, to any permutation of three speakers. These speakers are normally placed behind the set, left, right and up-centre, but they are all on long leads and can be moved to place sounds even more exactly. Now that, I admit, is a pretty elaborate set-up, but if I were asked to specify the minimum ideal equipment, then I would say you should have at least one tape-deck, one record player and three extension speakers. You should be able to record from the player onto the tape-deck and to play from either or both into any one or, if necessary, all three of the speakers simultaneously.

As a general rule I make a sound effects tape for every play, putting onto one reel, or sometimes two, all the sounds needed and separating each one from the next by inserting a strip of yellow leader tape. The stage-manager or assistant operating the equipment merely has to run the tape on cue, stopping it every time he comes to a leader, and to flick the switch that operates the appropriate speaker. One production we did opened on a room in semi-darkness. Before any dialogue occurred, there was a dog barking in the street, someone hammering in a room above, and a baby crying in another room. We placed a speaker underneath a window, right, another one up-stage, high up on the back of the set, and a third in the wings, left. As the tape ran, the stage manager switched first to the window speaker, right, then as the dog stopped barking he switched to the speaker up-centre, and when the hammering ceased, to the speaker left. From the audience's point of view, there was very obviously a street outside that window, clearly a room above the one they could see, and yet another one behind the wall on their right. The whole ambience was captured perfectly.

If you decide to follow my suggestion about making an effects tape, you may wonder how to obtain the sounds that you put on it in the first place. Well, in recent years several of the major commercial record companies have released LPs with a selection of sounds, but the very finest that I have encountered is a set of a dozen albums made in France and available in England at dealers who specialise in imports, or direct from Selecta in Southwark Bridge Road, London. The series is called *Audio-Camera* and is subdivided into sections on the sounds of nature, everyday life, and transport. There are superb recordings of all types of wind, rain and storm, wild animals and domestic animals, farm animals and machinery, electric mixers, coffee grinders, vacuum cleaners, and all manner of trains and boats and planes, not to mention cars, buses, carriages – and there is even one album on special sounds for space fiction. Several societies obtained sets of these records after hearing me demonstrate them on radio and to the best of my knowledge they are still available at the time of writing.

I should have added to the list of basic essentials a microphone, because I have often found the need to record some items myself. For instance, in Chekov's *Uncle Vanya* I was unable to find for the part of Telyegin an actor who could actually play the guitar, nor could I find on a commercial record exactly the guitar music that I wanted, so I brought in a very fine player and made a recording of him myself, Then again, on several occasions I have wanted the effect of a chorus singing off-stage, and as our wings are not large enough for this to be done live at performance, I have recorded the cast singing the songs.

There are still some sounds which are best produced live by the stage-manager, and among these is gunshot. Try as I might, and with the able assistance of BBC sound effects experts, I have never been able to record a revolver or rifle shot which reproduced realistically on stage. If a gun is to be fired on stage, in view of the audience, then I think you must obtain an accurate replica capable of firing blanks. There is no alternative, and all the substitutes that I have come across produce a risible effect. By the way, before you are even allowed to hire a practical gun for the stage, you must obtain a licence from the police and this can sometimes take quite a long time, so set things in motion well in advance. One more word of caution; if a gun is to be fired 'on' always see that the stage-manager has a substitute 'off'. Many actors will recount experiences of pulling a trigger at a dramatic moment, only to be met with a dull click because the blank is a dud. If the SM can, with a split second delay, fire an alternative gun it may not be totally realistic, but it can avert utter disaster.

I mentioned earlier the old-fashioned wind machine and thunder sheet, and these can still be used very satisfactorily. The wind machine is really just a fan, encased in a metal cage, and the velocity can be raised or lowered by means of a dial. This is ideal for a long scene in which wind is to be heard at varying intensity throughout, sometimes rising to a gale shriek on certain word cues. The SM has complete control on such occasions, and it is well nigh impossible to make a long recording which will time perfectly to dialogue. It only needs an actor to cut a line unwittingly, and the wind peaks will come in all the wrong places.

The thunder sheet is nothing more nor less than a large sheet of metal, suspended on cords and with a handle at the bottom. By grasping the handle and shaking the sheet it produces the most convincing booms and rumbles. It does have the disadvantage of occupying a fair amount of space, but again it is much easier to time effects with dialogue. This matter of precise timing raises the vexed question of just who should cue who. In many instances a sound has to follow an action rather than a word, so obviously the ideal situation is for the SM to have a full, uninterrupted view of the whole stage, but this is seldom practicable. It therefore follows that someone who *can* see the whole stage, most likely the prompter or the lighting technician, must give an electric cue to the person operating the sound effects. As I have explained earlier, my own lighting man is situated at the rear of the auditorium, and he gives a cue by means of flashing a low-powered red bulb over the sound console.

There are, oddly enough, some sounds which are more convincing when produced artificially than by the real thing. A good example is the click of a light switch. A real switch doesn't often make the sort of sound that one thinks a switch should make, but two coins, separated by the index finger and suddenly snapped together do. Don't ask me why. Another useful gadget can be made from an old bicycle pump or swannee whistle plunger, with a cork pushed into the end and attached to the barrel with a piece of string: perfect for simulating the pop of a champagne cork. Also, a cork rotated in french chalk in a saucer makes a beautiful creaking door or squeaking staircase. The list of tricks of the trade is a long one, but I would suggest that whenever a real sound doesn't seem right, then see what a little ingenuity can do with substitutes. Let me quote just one more example, though I can't think of many instances in which it might be required. We needed one one ocasion to have the sound of a head being chopped off, and falling from the block. As the 'real' thing was rather out of the question, we found that by whacking a heavy knife into a firm cabbage and then letting the cabbage drop to the floor we achieved an effect worthy of the long and blood-curdling tradition of grand guignol!

Returning to the subject of a sound effects tape, there is one procedure that a producer should always adopt. That is, to listen from the auditorium to each separate track, establishing as you go the correct volume level of reproduction. The SM should then mark those settings in his book alongside each effect – and do bear in mind that the level which seems right in an empty theatre will be too quiet when the theatre is full, because human bodies absorb sound and deaden it. The right balance is something that you can only learn to judge by trial and error and practical experience.

Falling into the same category as effects is incidental music. You will probably want to play music while the audience is gathering, and most plays are all the better for music at curtain up and frequently at act or scene curtains. I shall not even begin to attempt suggesting specific examples of music, for that choice should always be made by a producer and his choice should be determined by the dramatic effect he wants to achieve. But you must be quite clear about how you stand legally over the public reproduction of gramophone recordings. In some cases you will find that the hall or theatre you hire for performances is already in possession of a licence for phonographic performance rights which will cover you for any records you might wish to play, but if it is not, then you must obtain your own. If in any doubt at all, then I suggest you contact the London office of the Performing Rights Society, or the local representative of the NODA (National Operatic and Dramatic Association) who will be able to help you. You will find that you are only required to make a very small annual payment for such a licence, but remember that failure to do this could result in legal action against you.

Chapter 10

Voice Production and Diction

One can theorise about the technique of production and acting until the cows come home, and the free exchange of ideas certainly does more good than harm. Yet when it comes down to fundamentals, an actor has three 'tools of his trade' and they are his brain, his body and his voice. He uses his brain to understand his play, to use imagination and knowledge in the creation of a character, and then he must convey his thoughts to an audience by the movements and sounds that he makes. No pianist would attempt to play a concerto on a piano which had half its notes stuck down; no painter would face a canvas with a handful of brushes which were solid with dried paint, and no sculptor set about a block of stone with blunt chisels. Yet how many actors have the temerity to tread the boards with an untrained voice and a body that is, to say the least, ill-controlled! I therefore intend to devote this and the ensuing chapter to exercises, unrelated to any particular play, which can help us all to achieve greater flexibility and fluency in speech and movement. Let me say at the outset that there are complete works available on both subjects, and private teachers abound to help the serious student and would-be professional, but I propose to reduce matters to a few basics which should not encroach too much on the time available to the average amateur.

It will come as a surprise to most people to learn that in all probability they have been breathing incorrectly for the greater part of their lives. How on earth, they may well ask, can there be anything incorrect about an action so natural, performed without thinking about it since we were slapped on the bottom at birth? The fact is that over the years most of us fall into a lazy way of breathing, particularly those of us who follow sedentary occupations. If we spend the working day sitting down, then the chances are that we use very slight inhalations, taking in just enough air to keep alive, and this is known as 'shallow breathing.' Be completely honest with yourself and consider right now, quite deliberately and objectively, how you are breathing as you read these words. Now – take a deep breath, and hold it. Does it feel as though the upper part of the chest has expanded, and perhaps that the shoulders have risen slightly? Is there a stiffness, or constriction, about the neck, throat and shoulders? (All right, breathe out now!) If you had to answer 'yes' to either or both of those questions, then you were breathing incorrectly.

The opposite of 'shallow' breathing is, quite obviously 'deep' breathing, and a deep breath begins with an intake of air not to the top, but to the lower part of the lungs. Now, with the tips of the fingers, feel the bottom of your rib cage and you will find that the lowest ribs are more flexible than the others. They can be moved in and outwards with a muscular action and are known as the floating ribs. As you stretch them outwards as far as they will go, you will also experience a tightening sensation in the space between the ribs. This is the diaphragm which, when properly developed by the right exercises, will control your breathing and consequently your voice production.

With the finger tips still on the lower ribs, take a deep breath again and be conscious of the fact that while the floating ribs are moving outwards, the diaphragm is filling and expanding forwards. Hold the breath for a moment and then let it out as slowly as possible, feeling the diaphragm retract and the ribs come back to where they started. Repeat the exercise several times until you think that you are starting to be aware of the mechanics of correct breathing. After a time you will also be aware that you can control the slow exhalation of a deep breath over a considerable period by means of the diaphragm. Try to think about this several times during the course of each day. Whatever you are doing, analyse the way that you are breathing and if it is incorrect, then put it right. This is not something that will happen overnight. It will require long and frequent practice because, after all, you are trying to eradicate the bad habits of a lifetime. Fortunately, this is something we can all do during the working day, whatever our occupation, but you should also make a point of starting any session of voice production exercises with a few minutes of breathing exercises as already described. I can promise you that, given time and patience, the new method of breathing will become natural to you and you will do it without conscious thought. In fairness to figure-conscious ladies I should point out that constant practice enlarges the diaphragm and I have heard one or two actresses complain of the fact, but don't worry. You will be much more aware of the different feel than anyone else will be aware of a different appearance, and you should certainly not reach the proportions of a Teutonic soprano!

Having started to breathe correctly, we now turn our attention to the proper development of tone and of placing the voice correctly. This is known as projection, and is the art of speaking in such a way that, without shouting, the voice is audible over a considerable distance.

Try the following. This is not an exercise, and you will only need to do it once, but it will immediately illustrate the difference in sound of a tone wrongly, then more or less rightly, produced. Take a deep breath in the way we have learned then, while holding the breath, make a long 'ah' sound. You will, of course, *have* to let out some breath in order to make any sound at all, but feel as though you are holding it. The sound was flat and guttural and came, probably quite painfully, from the back of the throat, didn't it? Now go through the same procedure again except that this time, instead of attempting to hold the breath, let it out easily and slowly with complete control from the diaphragm. This time the 'ah' should have sounded much more open and round, and you should have felt that the tone was coming from further forward in the face – not squeezed back in the throat. Listen to the people whom you hear around you from day to day, not for what they are saying but the way in which they are saying it, and I guarantee you will hear more tones similar to the first sound you produced than to the second. Imagine playing a long role using that bad voice and I think you will agree that not only would it sound ugly, but it would place a great strain on the voice and you would be lucky if you could speak at all at the end of a week.

So clearly we have to concentrate on producing all the sounds we make from well forward and to give them what is known as 'frontal resonance.' Fortunately this is something we can feel we are doing perfectly correctly by physical sensation. First hum a long note and while you are doing it feel the bridge of the nose, the top of the cheeks and the bottom of the forehead with your fingers. Using only the lightest touch you will be aware of a distinct vibration in these areas from the bones covering the frontal cavities of the skull. It is *almost* impossible to hum from the back of the throat, but if you cannot feel the vibration I have mentioned continue the exercise and *think* the sound forward until you can. It will get there eventually. Having reached that stage, start off a note by humming and then open the mouth to make an 'ah' sound without a break so that the result will be 'Mmmmmmm-aaaaah.' You will probably find at first that as you open your mouth the sound will go back into the throat, but with practice it will stay almost as far forward as the humming and you will still be able to feel the vibration in the bones. This is really the basic technique of singing, but in time you will be able to retain the same tonal quality in spoken words.

Now we are not only breathing correctly, but also using that control to project sounds in the right way as well. Next we must consider the nature of those sounds.

Intelligible speech, in any language, consists of vowel sounds punctuated by consonants. By and large it is the vowels that give words their meaning and the consonants that add shape and definition. Leaving aside the special case of regional dialects, which is something we shall come to later on, *poor* speech is marked by badly produced vowels and the mis-use or complete failure to use consonants. Initially we must look at both ingredients separately.

If I ask you how many vowel sounds there are in speech you will probably reply, by reflex action, 'Five.' Grammatically, as applied to the written word, there are of course five vowels, but in the spoken word there are, or should be, no less than thirteen different and distinct vowel *sounds*. The only accurate way to convey these in print is by the use of phonetics, and the serious student of speech will really have to learn how to read them. However, that is beyond the scope of this chapter, so let us try a simpler method. Here is a sentence of thirteen words, quite meaningless, but employing the thirteen different sounds:

'Who would know ought of art must err and yet take his ease.'
For the purpose of the exercises which follow we must find a non-phonetic way of writing those thirteen sounds, so here are the vowels expressed in a different way. Look at each one in turn and relate them in the same sequence to the sentence above.

OO – U (closed) – O (long) – OR – O (short) – AH – U (open) – ER – A – EH – AY – i – EE.

Now eleven of those vowels are mono-tonal, consisting of one pure sound, but two of them are diphthongs, made up of two sounds: O (long) is made up of a very short ER quickly eliding into OO, and AY is compounded in the same way of EH and i. The written vowels i and u were not included in the sentence because they too are diphthongs, made up in turn of AH – EE and i – OO. So there we have all the sounds we need (consonants excluded) for good standard English speech.

Although the thirteen vowel-sounds sentence above has no meaning, it has been constructed in such a way that if the vowels are correctly produced you will begin with the mouth opened at the smallest aperture, with the lips pursed almost in a kiss, and with each succeeding vowel you will need to open the mouth just a little more until you reach the maximum point with the sound 'AH' (the word 'art'). From that point on the jaws begin to come together again slowly, but the mouth extends sideways until reaching the maximum 'photographer's smile' position at EE (the word 'ease'). With this in mind, run through the thirteen sounds again, noticing just how the mouth and jaws change position slightly with each change of vowel. If you find you are changing from any one to another without a discernible physical movement, then *one* of the vowels at least was incorrect. If you want to hear a demonstration of perfectly pronounced vowels as a guide, then I suggest you either buy or borrow a copy of any recording by Sir John Gielgud. There was a time when I might have advocated listening to almost any BBC news reader, but this is alas no longer the case. However, whatever means you use, once you are quite sure that you have the correct standard sounds perfectly in your head you can begin using them in exercises.

Since there are only two words in the English language made from one single vowel sound alone ('or' and 'are') we must now move on to the use of consonants. All but two of these, the hard G as in 'gate' and the aspirate H, are produced by movement of the lips, teeth and tip of the tongue, and not merely by the exhalation of breath over the vocal chords through a variable aperture (the mouth) as is the case with vowels. In fact in that last sentence there is a phrase which in itself is a good consonant exercise: 'lips, teeth, tip of the tongue.' Try repeating it over and over again, more and more quickly, and be acutely aware as you do so just how those features come into play as you say the words.

Now I am going to give you a few sequences of consonants which I want you to relate to the vowels we have already studied, taking them first each one in turn. The first sequence is M, N, L. Preface our first vowel, OO, with each consonant so that we have MOO, NOO, LOO, and then repeat the process with each of the other twelve vowels in our sentence. Try at the same time to apply everything we have learned so far, including breath control, forward projection of the vowels and frontal resonance. Now we can extend the exercise a stage further, incorporating several sounds at once, thus: MAH NAH LAH, MOR NOR LOR, MOO NOO LOO, MAY NAY LAY, MEE NEE LEE. Again, when you have grown accustomed to the sequence, accelerate the pace of delivery as much as you can. The great value of this high speed diction, which we shall return to again and again, is to develop elasticity in the organs of speech. If you can achieve total clarity with rapid delivery your enunciation will be perfect at a more normal pace.

You have enough material there to work on for several sessions of, say, half-an-hour at a time. If I were conducting personal speech classes I should certainly limit exercises to the few we have covered so far for a week or two. Don't try to rush the process, because, as I have said before, good speech is not something that can be learned overnight. Remember that even Henry Higgins took three months to turn Eliza into a Duchess!

The next step is to extend our sequence of consonants even further, so that it becomes M, N, L, V, TH, Z, and then follow the same procedure as before so that you will now be reciting: MAH NAH LAH VAH THAH ZAH, MOR NOR LOR VOR THOR ZOR, etc. If you find that straight repetition of these exercises gets a little boring, may I suggest that you try singing them to well known melodies? I discovered for example, that the one we have just been considering can be fitted with a little ingenuity to the famous Scherzo from the Litolff piano concerto.

There remain the so-called explosive consonants, which are all produced by building up air pressure behind the lips, the tip of the tongue, or at the back of the throat, and then suddenly releasing it: P, T, K, and then again, using first the lips and then the tongue, we have B and D. Exercises consist of following each of these with vowel sounds just as we did with the other consonants: PAH TAH KAH, PAY TAY KAY, PEE TEE KEE, or perhaps BAH DAH TAH, BAY DAY TAY and so on.

After a few sessions of exercises only, start putting these precepts into practice by declaiming poetry. You will obviously be able to find examples of your own, but let me make just one or two suggestions to try to indicate the sort of verse to look for.

The works of Tennyson, Masefield and Kipling are a veritable treasury of diction exercises, with their rhythmic application of vowel sounds, and the use of onomatopoeia and alliteration. Take for instance Tennyson's *The Beggar Maid*:

> As shines the moon in clouded skies,
>   She in her poor attire was seen:
> One praised her ankles, one her eyes,
>   One her dark hair and lovesome mien.
> So sweet a face, such angel grace,
>   In all that land had never been:
> Cophetua sware a royal oath:
> 'This beggar maid shall be my queen!'

That is a superb exercise for vowels – and for getting your lips, teeth and tip of the tongue round consonants, try this one from Kipling:

> And the talk slid north, and the talk slid south,
> With the sliding puffs from the hookah mouth.
> Four things greater than all things are, –
> Women and Horses and Power and War.

Then, for what is in effect a dramatic monologue, I would suggest Browning's *My Last Duchess*, and as that takes us back into the realms of drama which is, after all, our primary concern, you can move on to any of the great Shakespearean soliloquies.

From this point onwards you can really make up your own practice sessions, but it is advisable always to begin with breathing exercises, followed by those for intonation and resonance, rapidity of diction and then move on to a practical example. Always try to include one sample of high speed diction, and there is no more fruitful source for this than the work of W. S. Gilbert, for his lyrics were in many cases designed with exactly this kind of delivery in mind.

> Though the Philistines may jostle, you will rank as an apostle in the high aesthetic band,
> If you walk down Piccadilly with a poppy or a lily in your medieval hand.

Get round that little lot with clarity in five seconds flat and you'll be doing pretty well!

I have often heard criticism levelled at voice production and diction exercises on the grounds that they render the art of acting even more artificial than it need be, but I just simply do not agree. Once you have learned to ride a bicycle, you don't analyse the principles of balance, or think about the need to steer and rotate pedals every time you go for a spin. These things come automatically – but you had to learn how to do them in the first place. So with acting, it is not enough to recite a few lines and feel deep emotion within your own breast unless an audience can hear and understand those lines and you can communicate your feelings. When you play a role, you will not be aware of breath control, or resonance and projection, or of clarity of diction, but if you have worked hard at learning these techniques your performance will gain in stature and so will your audience's appreciation of it.

There is a story which I like to believe is true that Sir Laurence Olivier, renowned among many other virtues for his great clarity of diction at remarkable speed, used to practice with small pebbles in his mouth as an added difficulty. If he could be lucid with such an impediment, then how much better would he be without it.

Chapter 11

Movement on Stage

Anyone who has never acted may wonder, at first glance, why I saw fit to add the words 'on stage' to this chapter-heading. If those of us in full possession of our faculties who are fit and healthy go about the motions of our daily lives in reasonably graceful fashion, then surely, it is reasonable to suppose, we can be expected to behave in the same way on a stage. After all, in most cases we should only be required to sit, stand, walk about, and gesture freely with our hands. Alas, it is not quite so simple! Watch any performance by relatively inexperienced players, and you will see normal, healthy people adopting the most ungainly stances, moving about in a totally unnatural manner, and contorting their limbs in frightening fashion. The reason for this can be explained in one word – *tension*.

Tension on stage stems from a multitude of factors. I think that even if we have a burning desire to act, when we actually get onto a stage in front of an audience we are often overwhelmed with a sense of our own audacity. Those people out there have come along in good faith, have even paid money, to watch our skill in impersonation: to laugh, cry, or share some other deep emotion with us and to believe that we are really someone other than we are. Then there are all those words to remember which we are quite certain we shall forget. Just think of the horror of standing there, in public, not knowing what to say next but all too aware that the audience and the other actors are desperately waiting for you to get on with it. And what on earth does one do in everyday life with one's hands? They never seemed a cause of embarrassment before, yet up here on stage these giant, red appendages keep obtruding all the time.

With all those thoughts running through the mind, it is impossible to concentrate objectively on how one is standing or moving. Perhaps the body-weight goes onto one leg, leaving the other twisted awkwardly; the toes turn in or out, or one foot starts to twine round the other ankle. Shoulders hunch up and hands are either desperately locked in front of the body or else, more often, thrust deep into pockets.

Those are the symptoms and end-products of stage-fright. And unfortunately stage-fright is something that you are all going to experience at some time, for neither I nor anyone in the world can teach you how to overcome it completely. To tell the truth, after hundreds of performances, I still feel monstrous waves of nausea in the moments before going on stage. However, we can take measures to counteract the feelings to some extent and, more important, to ensure that we don't look nervous to an audience. Just as the root cause of the dilemma lay in tension, so the answer to the problem can also be given in one word – *relaxation*. Furthermore, we can actually learn to relax, and that is precisely what we must do before going on to exercises designed to develop fluidity of movement on stage.

Unlike voice production and diction exercises, the routine of relaxing is not something that can satisfactorily be done with a book in your hands, so I suggest that you absorb the full description of what to do before attempting to do it. It should perhaps also be emphasised that this again is something needing a great deal of practice, so don't expect any instant miracles, although you should be able to begin to experience the right kind of sensations from the start.

First, spend a couple of minutes in breathing exercises as detailed in the preceding chapter. Then lie down flat on your back, arms at the sides, and continue deep breathing for a while. Now take a really deep breath, hold it, and putting the arms out above the head stretch as hard as you can go. Push up with the hands and down with the feet until you feel every muscle in your body tighten up with the effort. Hold this for a second, then breathe out slowly, bringing the arms down loosely beside the body, palms downwards, and letting the whole body go limp.

Repeat this three or four times, each time trying to be sure that when you go limp there is no muscular tightness anywhere in the body.

Now, as you lie in this relaxed position, go round the whole body, mentally, checking each point as you go. It sometimes helps to imagine a ball being inserted into the sole of one foot, running up the leg and the side of the body, through the shoulder and down the arm to the hand, back up again, across the shoulders and neck, down the other arm and back, down the other side of the body and leg, and out again through the other foot. Take all the time you need over this, really feeling each area to be completely relaxed before moving on to the next. Tell yourself that the sole of the left foot is loose and limp, that there is no tension in the toes or the ankle. Now move up to the left calf, and feel that it is loose and flabby. Think away all tension in the knee, and so to the left thigh. The hip joint is next, and you should concentrate until you actually feel this open up and fall back, as though the whole of the left leg were rolling away. So on up to the shoulder, which is generally a great area of tension and may take quite a time and great concentration to relax, and then down through the muscles of the upper arm and forearm, to the wrist. Even your fingers must each, individually, feel loose and free from strain.

Back again to the shoulder, move your attention across now, thinking about the neck muscles, into the right shoulder, and so on, in reverse order down to the toes of the right foot. Now see if the spine still feels rigid and try to relax there also, and don't forget the face. Let your mouth and cheeks go loose, and make your brow serene and free from wrinkles.

Finally, when the whole body feels completely relaxed, imagine yourself lying on a warm, sunny beach, absolutely at ease and your mind reposed. Imagine that the body, which you can scarcely feel at all, is drifting away and you are totally happy. You will find that your breathing, which you had completely forgotten about, has slowed right down and you will probably be taking slow, small intakes of air. The motionless, fully-relaxed body needs considerably less oxygen than is consumed by tension and vigorous activity. After a few minutes, come back to earth, sit up and finally stand.

Apart from being a thoroughly pleasant exercise to perform,

this is fascinating to do as a group. Take it in turns to have one member giving the instructions, more or less as I have described them here, for this will take away even the effort of having to think what you are doing. Also, the instructor, or observer, will be able to see physical changes quite plainly in the rest of you as you relax.

I recommend a few minutes spent in this way every day, if possible, and you will find that a couple of minutes of total relaxation is as much a restorative as several hours relatively uncomfortable sleep. If you really persevere with this exercise you will eventually reach the stage at which it is unnecessary to go through the lengthy process of 'thinking' each part of the body relaxed in turn, and will be able to go into a totally limp state instantly. Having mastered the art, you will also find that a minute or two spent breathing properly, and then totally relaxed, will ease your mind immeasurably just before going on stage.

Relaxing properly is the main key to graceful movement on stage, but almost equally important is absolute physical control and total awareness of what various limbs are doing. This is something that will come gradually, and there are a few simple exercises that can help. These are not designed to promote muscular development like normal P.T., though they may do that incidentally. The aim is rather at fluidity of movement and control of the limbs – at awareness of what hands, arms, legs and feet are doing without actually looking to see.

1. It is useful to learn first of all the five basic foot positions used in ballet, and they are as follows. Stand all the time straight and relaxed and then, one: with heels together, turn the feet outwards at right-angles to the front of the body; two, with feet still at the same angle, slide the left foot to the side; three, still keeping the feet turned outwards, slide the right foot in until the heel is against the left instep; four, move the right foot directly forward about eighteen inches, but still keep it at right angles to the body; five, bring the right foot in again to the body, but this time so that both feet are side by side, heel to toe, and both feet still turned outwards. It may be a little difficult to retain your balance, in some positions at first, so by all means stand beside a chair with the right hand resting on the back of it for support.

Once you have learned the basic positions, the exercise is to do knees bend four times in each of them. Then relax.

2. Now kneel on one knee and with your hand force the other knee outwards and to the side, opening up the hip. Do this three or four times, then change over and repeat with the leg on which you were previously kneeling.

3. Standing beside your chair, swing the outside leg forwards and backwards about eighteen times, then from the standing position swing it out sideways the same number of times, and finally swing backwards and forwards, pointing a figure of eight with the toe. Then turn round and repeat all these exercises with the other leg.

4. Now concentrate on the hips, pelvis and base of the spine. Standing upright, with feet slightly apart, bend the torso forward and down, away to the left and back up to the upright position. This should be done in one, smooth, circular motion about eight times. Then repeat the exercise, swinging away and up to the right.

5. Still standing, legs apart, place the hands on the bottom of the ribs and throughout this exercise try to ensure that the upper part of the body remains quite motionless. Now rotate the hips and pelvis in a swinging circular movement, first in one direction, then in the other. As a variation to this exercise, keep the lower part of the body still, and, above the line of the stomach move the upper part of the body, from the rib cage up, outwards first to the left and then to the right.

6. Next we move on to the shoulders. In a standing position, push the shoulders forwards, then raise them and push them backwards, then lower to the normal stance. Do this about eight times.

With arms held out at the side of the body, press the shoulder blades together. Then, keeping them together, move the arms forwards, then relax first the left shoulder blade, then the right. This should be done four times.

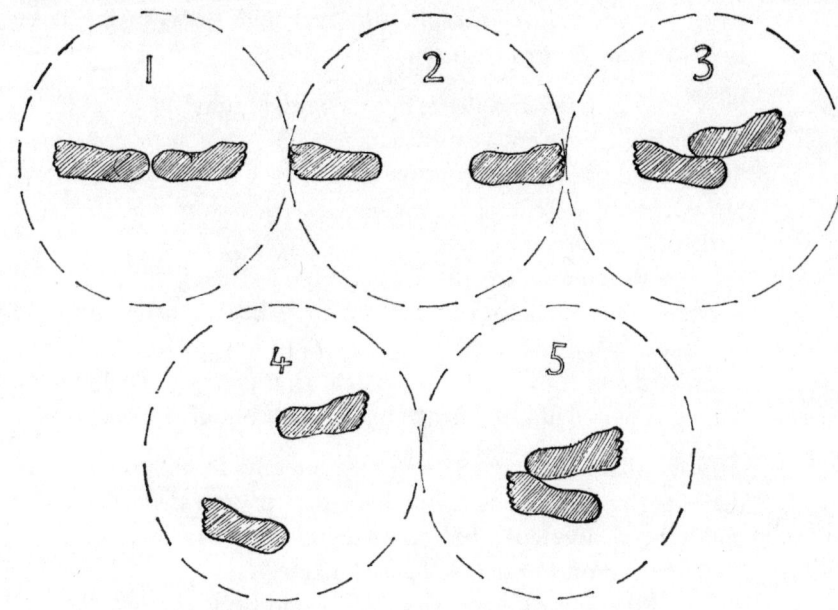

Fig. 12 Basic ballet positions

It will certainly do no harm to add other exercises which you probably know already and which are more in the nature of callisthenics, for acting needs great stamina and fitness is almost a prerequisite. However, the simple routine I have described was designed, as I have said, to help you make your movements more relaxed yet at the same time controlled.

There are in addition a number of group activities which can be of immense help to any dramatic society, and although most of them fall outside the scope of this book they should perhaps at least be mentioned. For example, dancing. We used the five basic ballet positions in our exercises, but if you can find someone with more advanced training to take your group in simple ballet classes you will find them both useful and enjoyable. You should certainly try to learn some period dances, such as the Pavane, Galliard, Gavotte and the Minuet, for sooner or later you will want to feature one of them in a play. Shakespeare makes constant reference to the dance, and in most cases the action should suit the word. Consider, for example, this exchange between Sir Toby Belch and Sir Andrew Aguecheek:

Sir T.: What is thy excellence in a galliard, knight?
Sir A.: Faith, I can cut a caper.
Sir T.: And I can cut the mutton to it.
Sir A.: And, I think, I have the back-trick simply as strong as any man in Illyria.
Sir T.: Wherefore are these things hid? wherefore have these gifts a curtain before them? are they like to take dust, like Mistress Mall's picture? why dost thou not go to church in a galliard and come home in a coranto? My very walk should be a jig; I would not so much as make water but in a sink-a-pace.

Now that little scene, presented merely as an exchange of dialogue, is well enough, but interspersed with deftly executed and *correct* dance steps it becomes a delight.

At the end of *As You Like It*, the Duke says:
'Play music! – and you, brides and bridegrooms all,
With measure heap'd in joy, to the measures fall.'
While at the end of *A Midsummer Night's Dream* two dances are called for, first a 'Bergomask' from the rude mechanicals who have just presented their play before the Duke, and then a song and dance for Oberon, Titania and the fairies.

Since those three comedies are possibly the ones most performed by amateurs, I think they prove my point.

Fencing, too, is not only a magnificent sport but of inestimable use to an actor. Stage-fights are a subject I intend to return to in a later chapter, and are indeed something that should never be attempted by the inexperienced without instruction, but even women, who are seldom required to fight with swords on stage, will find that fencing helps them enormously in poise and movement. An actor in my own group has recently started to attend evening classes for fencing and thoroughly endorses everything I have said in this respect.

So, finally, to mime. This is at once the very root of acting, and yet the one area that most amateurs and a great many professionals feel most unhappy about. It is nowadays, certainly in European theatre, a highly specialised branch of the art and, developed to its highest level, only seen in the ballet or in solo performances by a few brilliant artists. There is no need for us to attempt to reach such a stage and yet I am convinced that we should all be much more aware of mime than we are. In almost any play you care to think of there will be moments in which the skilful actor can reveal a great deal about himself and his surroundings, entirely without the use of words, and solely by his movements. The needs of each play, and each character, will of course be different, but there is a type of exercise we can practise as a group that will heighten appreciation of the validity of this point and also sharpen imagination. I am going to give you a few imaginary situations, and I suggest that as a group exercise, you work through these and invent others for yourselves. Each member in turn should take one example, and try to convey the situation to the others completely without the use of words but solely by movement or, if you like, mime.

1. You are on a beach, sunning yourself – you are alone – you are a vain, conceited person. You hate cold water and swimming, but it is the fashion, so you decide to go into the shallow water and show yourself off. However brave you try to be, when your feet touch the water you can't keep it up for long, and when a huge wave suddenly soaks you completely your self-control and desire to show off leave you.

2. You are a thief. You go into a hotel (make the location clear, suggesting corridors, doors, etc.,) and enter a room. The room is in darkness. You try to find your way about, discover a chest of drawers, steal something, then escape.

3. You are a fat character. You try to get into a tube-train during rush hour. There is a hold up on the line, the tube gets very hot, and you suffer from the heat and anxiety. Then at last the train moves off.

4. You go for a walk, see a butterfly, and try to catch it. You succeed, and enjoy looking at it. Then it escapes and you try to catch it again, growing more and more desperate. Then you trip and fall.

5. You are in the country and run to catch a bus that you see arriving in the distance. You wave to the driver, then suddenly trip over a barbed-wire fence and your clothes get caught. The bus stops, but the driver does not see you. You get more and more entangled as the bus drives away.

Now if you look at each of those situations carefully, you will see that you are not only asked to tell a story in movement only, but to indicate such details as your physique, exactly where you are, your character and the weather. Then you will also have to make an audience *see* the other objects with which you come in contact. I cannot possibly tell you, by means of the written word, how to tackle each problem, for you can only find the answers by practice and the constructive criticism of your colleagues. However, there are three main aspects you should bear in mind. First, you must totally believe in your character and the situation. There are no words and no scenery to hide behind, and you will never convince others by what you are doing unless you have first convinced yourself. Second, remember that mime does not only involve use of the hands. You can convey a great deal by skilful use of the eyes. Really *see* the size, shape and dimension of objects if you want to make others see them as well. Finally, when you are handling anything, be very conscious of the weight of it, and how that would affect your general stance. A common fault when starting mime is to pick up, say, a chair in a manner in which it would appear to be as light as the butterfly in exercise 4.

In this chapter I have, I know, suggested various activities which there would never be time to get round to in the general course of a production. But a dramatic society grows in stature, and really becomes a society if between productions you organise group evenings that are not just social gatherings, or fund-raising events, but are in effect classes in drama. Teachers can help enormously, beyond doubt, but as I said right at the beginning of the book, the best way to learn about acting is to act. I would now add that the next best thing is to practise various facets of the art as often and as seriously as you can.

Chapter 12

Advice to the Players

Before writing a word of this chapter I have been reading once again that remarkable scene in *Hamlet* in which he addresses the group of actors about to perform before his uncle, the King. This is at the beginning of Act III scene ii, and if you are unfamiliar with the work, then I do recommend you most strongly to study these few lines. The amazing thing is that, although written nearly four hundred years ago, the advice contained therein is as pertinent now as it was then. Styles in acting and in writing plays may change, yet certain fundamentals remain constant, distinguishing good acting from bad.

In preceding chapters we have analysed briefly some of the mechanics of acting: how to improve speech and movement, how to study a play, then a part within that play, and how to learn that part. There still remain the little niceties which can add polish to a performance and for the most part these involve a knowledge of technique. Let it be said once again, any play can be presented in a variety of ways and no one should ever state categorically that one way is right and another wrong. The style in which a play is produced and the interpretation of a character in the play are matters in which the individuals concerned at the time are perfectly entitled to their opinions. If you have seen two actors give very different interpretations of the same role, you may have preferred one, but it doesn't follow that the other was wrong. Nevertheless, there are ways of doing some things both in acting and in production that are quite definitely wrong, beyond question, and it is some of these that we are going to consider now.

I have not mentioned so far, in suggestions for aspiring producers, the all important matter of sight-lines. These are the imaginary lines from any seat in the auditorium determining the area of the stage that can actually be seen from that seat. There are very few theatres in which that area is virtually the same from every point in the audience, and for that reason it is a grave mistake for a producer to work all the time from a position in the centre of the stalls. He may establish the placing of a group of actors on stage that looks fine from his vantage point, but is quite confusing from the point of view of a member of the audience sitting at the side. For example, let us suppose that you have a scene in which one character has most of the dialogue and he has been placed up stage centre (UC), while several other players, listening to him are spread out diagonally to down left (DL) and down right (DR). It is quite possible that, viewed from say the extreme ends of the front row, the speaker will be concealed, or 'masked' from sight. Or alternatively, imagine a scene in which there is a balcony set up stage and on which some characters are to appear. They may be perfectly visible from the first few rows, but perhaps from the back of the hall their heads are obscured by the top of the proscenium arch. In such a case, either the actors on the balcony would have to lean forwards over a balustrade, or the balcony be lowered or the idea scrapped altogether. But my point is that, having set his play, the producer should wander about during some rehearsals, watching scenes from every angle and readjusting his grouping if necessary to ensure that everything can be seen from every seat.

Having said all that, it should be stressed that the actors have an equal responsiblity to the audience to make sure that they adhere to the positions and moves which have been established by the producer. Perhaps this seems so obvious as to be scarcely worth mentioning, and yet I cannot remember how many times I have seen actors carelessly, or unwittingly, mask themselves behind other players. A two-handed scene seldom produces problems of this kind, but when there is a group on stage everyone in that group should take stock from time to time of relative positions. If you are placed up stage and find that someone has moved in front of you, then try to change your position, in a natural way, so that you are unmasked. Of course, you should be tremendously involved in the part you are playing, but not to the total exclusion of awareness of the audience. You are acting for them, not for yourself. If they cannot see you and appreciate your skill you are wasting your time.

The sort of move I have just described should, of course, only be used with discretion, as a corrective. It could be employed, and frequently was at one time, as a means of gaining ascendancy by one actor over another. Obviously someone well up stage and speaking dialogue is most likely to be at the focal point for the audience, while those down stage are almost obliged to turn round, backs to audience, to listen. There are legendary stories of big stars playing a scene together, and alternately easing up stage of each other in this way to hold the attention of the audience, and to hell with the dramatic requirements of the play. It doesn't happen so much today, though strangely enough the practice has given a phrase to common usage much employed by tabloid journalists: as I write this, Maria Callas has just given her first public concert for a number of years and actress Elizabeth Taylor caused a minor sensation by arriving a trifle ostentatiously twenty minutes late. One headline I noted read 'La Divine upstaged by Liz.' The sub-editor responsible clearly knew what he meant, but I wonder if he knew the origin of his phrase? (Incidentally, the practice is equally ill-mannered *on* stage.)

Following on from that, it is perhaps worth pointing out to actors and producers that it is by no means always necessary for one character to look at another, whether speaking or listening. In fact it is often more realistic and sometimes more dramatically effective to avoid doing so, though once again I should stress that the technique is to be used with discretion. I once employed it to excess myself, playing an entire role facing downstage, which resulted in a press notice remarking, 'Mr. Matthew appeared to find something extremely interesting in the proscenium arch, for he spent the whole evening looking at it.'!

There is one guiding principle that should never be ignored with reference to moves on stage, and this again is of equal importance to actor and producer. No move is justifiable unless it can be logically motivated. Perhaps you remember that I said in an earlier chapter it is a mistake when setting a play to follow printed move directions blindly, for they were geared to a set that was probably quite different from yours. Furthermore, it is never sufficient to move a character from one side of the stage to the other solely because he needs to be there a little later on. You must always consider *why* a person in the situation would want to move to a different position, and if no motivation is provided in the text, then invent one with a bit of business that is logical and appropriate. It might be a simple thing like crossing to a cigarette box or lighter, or fetching a pair of spectacles, glancing at a book, pouring a drink, and so on. Clearly you have to work out something that is appropriate to the scene and the action, and it must be totally credible or you defeat the object of the exercise. Skilfully invented business not only motivates moves, but it also thereby adds realism and helps an actor to remember.

A combined move that often seems to have a fatal attraction for the inexperienced, yet one that should always be avoided is known as 'the scissors'. This occurs when two characters cross each other on stage simultaneously. You will often find that the end-product of such a move is necessary, but it must always be achieved in a more subtle way. Let one actor complete his move across stage first, then the other can go in the opposite direction. The reason why the scissors is wrong is that it diverts the attention of the audience. They can only focus clearly on one move on stage at a time, so that two sharply positive changes of position occurring at the same time cause a split in interest and are extremely irritating to watch. It is just conceivable that a scirrors cross might be justifiable in one of those bedroom farces in which characters are always popping in and out of various doorways, but I can think of no other situation in which it should ever be used.

Another problem that often arises and one that can absorb a great deal of time at detail rehearsals is that of timing dialogue and movement together. There are no really hard and fast rules about this, but there are one or two factors it might be useful to bear in mind. The whole thing was aptly summed up in the Hamlet speech I referred to at the beginning of the chapter: 'Suit the action to the word, the word to the action.' Or to put that another way, don't let either actions or words get in each other's way. If you have an elaborate bit of business to complete during dialogue, be aware of the value of pausing both in what you are saying and in what you are doing. Never coincide a complicated action with a punch line, be it comic or dramatic, for once again you will be asking the audience to divide their attention and you will lose the effect of both. The pause in either word or movement can be fractional, but it must be made. A good example of this sort of thing is to be found in the first scene of the famous Ben Travers' farce *Rookery Nook*. The two cousins, Gerald and Clive Popkiss, have a long exchange of amusing dialogue while unpacking a portmanteau, pouring out glasses of whisky, one large and one small which constantly get swapped around, playing with a tie, a dressing gown and a loofah, and frequently bumping into each other. Now this scene has to be played at a cracking pace, and the audience should certainly not be aware at any time of pauses which would hold up the flow, but nevertheless those pauses must be there, to allow the visual and verbal jokes to get across. The two actors playing this scene will need to rehearse over and over again until the timing is absolutely right and firmly fixed in their minds.

For similar reasons you will find that it is often quite difficult to get a line of dialogue right while simply walking across a room, or sitting on a chair. This is not an unbreakable rule to be observed at all times, but you may find that it helps to pace the speech with pauses for the action. I often tell actors not to 'tread on' a line or not to 'sit on' it, but this is only a generalisation to bear in mind. Consider each situation as it arises on its own merits.

Then again, many beginners have an alarming tendency to lean on furniture. They will grasp at the back of a chair or the edge of a table like a drowning man at a straw, as though the sheer physical contact shomehow gives them moral support. Clearly there will be instances when the producer will ask an actor to lean on the back of a chair or on a table, to create the picture that he wants, but it all comes down to that same factor which should govern all moves, motivation. Put at its simplest, if there is a reason for the action, then that action is probably right. If there is no reason, then it is certainly wrong.

Now a word or two about something that frequently holds terror for many of us, and that is the stage-fall. There is no need to suggest a specific example, for we have all seen or read plays in which someone is either punched, stabbed, shot or poisoned and has to fall full-length on the stage. There is most definitely a right and wrong way to go about this particular action. The wrong way may not only look ludicrous, often causing unwanted laughter, but it can prove highly dangerous for the actor concerned. I have more than once taken a bad fall due to carelessness on my own part and had to play the rest of a scene in agony. Another actor of my acquaintance once fell in the wrong direction, struck his head and knocked himself unconscious and was unable to play the rest of the scene at all!

Stage-falls can be practised out of context and should be dealt with from time to time at exercise sessions. The two main things to bear in mind are that you should not fall in a heavy way which can give a sudden jar to knee, spine or wrist, and you must contrive the fall so that you know exactly where and in what position you are going to land. For a start, stand in the middle of the room with plenty of space around you. There should be no obstacle anywhere within the radius of your own height. Stand upright, as relaxed as possible, with the legs fairly close together. Now let yourself go sideways, fairly slowly, either to left or right, in a relaxed rolling motion, so that first your knee touches the ground, then the thigh and finally, the side of the body and shoulder. To complete the move, roll over onto your back or your stomach. At first you will find that you go down in a series of jerks, but continue to practise until you can fall in one smooth continuous move and always follow the sequence of knee, thigh, side. The next step is to learn to place the prostrate body precisely, falling either forwards or backwards. Still start the fall in the same way, but after the knee makes contact with the floor start to sway the body in the appropriate direction so that when the thigh touches you are moving into the required position. These are the basic mechanics of the technique of falling, but of course the style of fall will change with the dramatic circumstances. A gentle swoon must look quite different from a fall resulting from a revolver shot at close range, but the difference will come from the trimmings that you add to the basic moves.

Should you ever have to fall down a flight of stairs, the same fundamental rules apply, but it calls for courage and confidence. I once shared a top-floor flat with a burly actor, now quite well known, who specialised in this sort of rough stuff and he would often scare me out of my wits by hurling himself headlong down the stairs to the landing below without apparent harm. I don't recommend the exercise, but I do underline the thinking behind it. If you have got to make a fall of any kind then do practise it over and over again until it is both convincing and safe.

Stage-falls will often be the outcome of stage-fights and since these will usually be with either fists or swords let us consider them separately. One thing is common to both, however, and that is the need for a sequence of moves to be learned and practised with total accuracy by both contestants. Fights should be completely choreographed with no room for improvisation. A mental lapse in dialogue can be harmlessly covered with an *ad lib*, but a mental lapse in a fight could prove lethal.

I must admit at the outset that a fist fight is the hardest thing to produce convincingly on stage and short of delivering real punches there is no way of achieving complete effectiveness. Unfortunately, modern audiences are so used to violent action on both film and television, where the real thing is so much easier to fake, that they will not be taken in by blows delivered off target. However, there are a couple of useful bits of technique that we can employ. The first and most difficult is the pulled punch – which calls for greater confidence on the part of the recipient than the deliverer. The term is probably self-explanatory, and means that a punch is thrown realistically, with force, but the blow is checked instantly at point of contact. A useful way of practising this is to punch the open palm of your opponent held up beside his shoulder. Now two things give credence to a blow. One is the sound that it makes and the other is the reaction of the person who has received the punch. The first can be achieved by the striker placing his own left hand against the jaw of his opponent and then throwing a pulled punch into it. The contact will make a fair old whack, and the left hand must then be withdrawn very quickly. If this is carried out with the attacker facing upstage, so that the mechanics are concealed from the audience, the result can be surprisingly effective. The illusion is completed by the reaction of the one who has apparently received the blow. The important thing for him to remember is that he must not anticipate the move and flinch before the actual contact. He could either make the whole thing look ridiculous or, more seriously, wind up on the receiving end of a punch before it had been pulled. If a fight consists of an exchange of blows, then do work out the whole sequence to the last detail and go through the moves slowly and often before trying to introduce elements of realism.

Sword fights on stage are much more commonly called for, but it would take more space than I have available to go into detail on the technique for these. I should just like to make the point that you are not going to get away with haphazard slashing away and clashing of swords, with the *coup de grace* delivered by one character thrusting his blade under the other's armpit! The most commonly-used weapons are foil, epée and sabre and each has its individual style with accepted positions and moves of attack and defence. For every thrust there is an appropriate and recognised parry, and so on. It is obvious therefore that while a real fight depends on the improvisation of combinations of these moves, a stage-fight – even quite a long one – can be worked out in absolute detail. If there is no one in your society who has had training in this sport, it is essential for you to co-opt the services of an experienced teacher. You will probably find that there are evening classes somewhere in your neighbourhood and it might be possible to persuade the instructor to come along to some of your rehearsals as a fight director.

In our production of *Hamlet*, which I have mentioned elsewhere, the actor playing Laertes and I spent days in a large garden away from the rest of the cast rehearsing our fight over and over again. It included some very spectacular sequences which we were able to make quite exciting with safety. When we rejoined the other actors for the first time they confessed that they were genuinely frightened by the realism, but of course we each had confidence that we knew precisely what the other was going to do next and how we were going to deal with it. On the other hand, I was once playing Toby Belch in a production of *Twelfth Night* and the actor playing Antonio, the sea captain, was a large and rather erratic gentleman who got carried away during our fight and started to introduce moves out of sequence. Thanks to excellent tuition by a fencing master I was able to cope with most of them, but one unexpected overhead swipe brought the point of his sword down between my eyes. Fortunately it only broke the skin on the bridge of my nose, but I still go cold when I think what might so easily have happened. So, if you have to be involved in a sword fight, make sure that it is properly worked out and supervised by an expert, then practise until you know the sequence backwards. First go through the moves slowly, and gradually increase the speed and the venom.

One final point on the subject of fights of any kind, and this raises a problem that I confess I am personally still struggling with after many years. At the height of passion, it is still desirable to be relaxed both physically and vocally, while giving the outward appearance of being perhaps angry and tense. If you fail to do this, as I invariably do, you will find that strain on the voice becomes quite painful and physical effort becomes more than necessarily tiring. There is no short cut to the ideal and it can only be achieved by great mental effort during rehearsals and performances. Whatever you are saying or doing, you must at all times will yourself to relax. You will probably fail, but it is worth the effort. It is imperative not to fail, however, where the fight takes the form of a struggle rather than the exchange of blows. If you have your opponent in a fierce half-nelson, held on with force, while he is striving equally strenuously to escape, you will both stagger about the stage uncontrollably and visually the result will be a mess.

So much for mortal combat. Let us consider now a few relatively peaceful aspects of acting that can still give rise to problems. First, playing to the lights. In a run-of-the-mill play with naturalistic setting this should not cause any worry, since the producer and lighting technician will have arranged the spots to give the actors broad illumination in all the main acting areas. But in a more stylised production, where single spots are used in surrounding darkness, it is essential that the player supposed to be in the spot should actually *be* in it. You can tell roughly from the stage, by looking at the spot, that you are more or less in its orbit, but if the beam is a narrow one it is impossible to tell whether you have found the centre of it. This can only be established at a dress rehearsal by someone in the auditorium. Once your position, relative to the light has been fixed you must make quite certain that you find exactly that position in performance. Not long ago I watched a young man playing a long scene supposedly in moonlight, during which he leaned awkwardly against the flats at the side of the stage while the 'moon' spot illuminated an area beside him but left his face in semi-darkness. He could have corrected this by moving half a pace to one side but failed to recognise the need and ruined the scene.

It may not always be possible for the actor who is supposed to be in the spot to get there without the help of fellow players. This lesson was brought home sharply to me many years ago when playing a minor part in an Old Vic production of *Henry V*. In the scene where Henry appears incognito among his troops on the eve of battle, I was one of a group of soldiers sprawled about a camp fire, centre stage. Henry stood in the middle of us, with his face illuminated by two front-of-house spots to simulate the glow from the fire. At the first dress rehearsal I had positioned myself incorrectly and during Henry's long speech I was mortified to receive a sharp kick up the back-side, accompanied by the un-Shakespearean words, 'Get out of my bloody light!'. I never made that mistake again.

There are, of course, ways of 'stealing the lime-light' from principals that have been used from time immemorial by supporting players, though it is a lamentable practice. One method is to wear a ring with a large cut stone in it, and by manipulation to pick up the reflection of a spot in one of the stone's facets. The flashing effect is bound to draw the audience's attention away from whoever is speaking at the time, to the detriment of the scene. I am sure that anyone reading this book will be sufficiently interested in acting to despise such an anti-social ploy, but if, as stage-manager or producer, you should catch some philistine in the act you might perhaps take steps to see that they don't get away with it again.

On the subject of supporting roles, it is perhaps worth mentioning that while it is obviously wrong to attempt to steal a scene, thereby upsetting the balance, it is at all times essential to remember that one is *in* the scene, and therefore in character. If one is sitting or standing somewhere on stage during a long exchange of dialogue by other players, it is necessary to retain the physical characteristics and the personality of one's own role. To react to what they are saying and doing in the way that that character would react. All too often one sees players who only seem to slip into their part when they are actually speaking and then become themselves again when silent. Remember, too, to start acting before you actually get on stage. You should really be the character you are playing in the wings, long before you enter, so that you make your entrance in character and don't assume it some seconds after you are on. I find it a great help to concentrate on the part I am playing from the moment I start to make up, and for that reason I hate dressing room chatter. Unfortunately, most of the amateurs with whom I have worked don't seem to share this point of view and often natter away until the moment they go on, but I honestly believe that this can lessen the impact of an appearance and, worse, increase the danger of missing an entrance altogether.

It is possible sometimes to be in danger of missing an entrance through no fault of one's own. The greatest hazard lies in the quick costume change that is occasionally called for both in modern and classical plays. A well-constructed play will usually have some action on stage of sufficient duration to cover the change, but a producer might just possibly reduce its effectiveness. For example, at the end of *As You Like It* Rosalind, in boy's attire, leaves the stage to reappear a little later in woman's clothes. Now Shakespeare, master craftsman that he was, introduces at that point a short scene between Touchstone, Jaques and the Duke, of just the right length. Unfortunately, the clown's two long speeches consist of jokes so archaic that they are unintelligible to a modern audience. The last time I produced the play I kept in his first speech but felt obliged to cut the second, thereby cutting Rosalind's changing-time dangerously. My wife, who was playing the part, complained that I had made it impossible, but in performance she managed to cope. This sort of situation underlines the point I made earlier about the necessity of having either costumes or something to represent them for rehearsals. Quick changes, like everything else connected with acting, are much easier after a little practice.

As a further illustration of this point, some years ago I made my one and only appearance in a professional pantomime, as Idle Jack in *Dick Whittington*. Now a traditional feature of all pantomimes is the **walk** down, or grand finale, in which all the characters take their **bows** resplendent in glamorous costumes worn only for that one entrance. In this particular production the last scene before the walk down was a comedy routine featuring Jack and the Dame. At the end of the scene there was a chorus number which ran on into the walk down, with all the supporting roles coming on first. The actor playing Dame and I had just over two minutes to rush to our dressing room, go through a complete change of costume and get back on again. At the first dress rehearsal, we both screamed to the producer that it was impossible, but he had been through all this before and told us to get on with it. To our utter amazement on the first night we managed to change. But by the end of the run, some weeks later, we were able to complete the change *and* drink a bottle of beer in the time that was left. Apart from practice, the only things you can do to facilitate a quick change are to make sure that the new costume is laid out as accessibly as possible, with any accoutrements such as rings, jewellery, belts, swords and so on easily to hand and visible, and to work out the easiest and fastest sequence of change.

Recalling that pantomime reminds me of another little piece of incidental information that I picked up which has since had an application in a straight play. There was the inevitable 'custard pie' routine, in which we hurled plates apparently piled high with whipped cream into each other's faces. On enquiry, I found that this substance was made by grating up finely a stick of ordinary shaving soap, tipping the parings into a pan containing a small amount of boiling water, continuing to boil until most of the water had evaporated, and then whisking the remains up into a mountain of foam. Sometime later I was involved in a production of R. C. Sherriff's celebrated World War One drama *Journey's End* in which one of the officers makes an entrance from his dug-out half-way through the process of shaving, his face covered in soap. He asked me how he could do this without ruining his make-up. The answer was to smear on a handful of the foam prepared as described, and without the use of conventional brush and water. It could then be scraped with a razor, and wiped off with a towel, without damage to the grease-paint and powder underneath. At drama school I was taught to cope with this problem by using whipped up white of egg which would no doubt work, but I have never tried it and rather suspect that the result might be a bit smelly!

By the way, if you think of using the foam for the first purpose I mentioned, the custard-pie routine, do be sure to tell anyone on the receiving end to keep his mouth shut. I once swallowed a lump of it and choked so badly that I couldn't speak for a couple of minutes. Fortunately, the Dame *ad-libbed* around the situation admirably and the audience enjoyed my discomfort as much as 'she' did, but I don't recommend the experience for the sake of a laugh.

Chapter 13

Front of House Management

We have so far discussed the presentation of plays from the point of view of those actively involved in production and performance. But no matter how hard these people work, much of their efforts will be wasted without the support of a team of devoted, self-effacing colleagues to ensure that everything runs smoothly. It therefore seems to me that it may be useful at this stage to consider how help can best be given by those who are neither actors nor, in the strict sense, back-stage workers.

Let us assume that we have a complete cast for a chosen play, rehearsing under their producer assisted by his stage-manager, and that the making of scenery and costumes is in hand, while the lighting technician also has his side of production under control. What else is needed before the play is ready to be presented before the public? It may well be that the activities I intend to outline in this chapter will be undertaken as secondary duties by some of those just mentioned, but ideally they are best handed over to people with nothing else to worry about.

First, I would recommend wherever possible the appointment of a production secretary. There is no reason why this job should not be combined with that of society secretary and indeed it could add interest to the chores of general administration. For instance, it is a great help if the production secretary can attend as many rehearsals as possible so that problems arising then can be taken in hand at once.

Once performance dates have been decided it is a good idea to confirm a booking for the hall you are going to use. Forgive me for over-stating the obvious, but I have known instances when a play has been well into rehearsal only to be postponed or cancelled when it was discovered that the hall was solidly booked up. As a matter of fact, I have frequently found that village halls have to accommodate so many varied activities that it is necessary to book all proposed performance dates a year in advance, which rather underlines a point I made earlier about the desirability of planning a whole season ahead.

Next, the secretary must apply for the licence to perform, where this is necessary. If you are working from a published acting edition, information about performing rights is included in the text and quite often the actual royalty payable is stated. In this connection, I should just point out that if your hall is a very small one with a total capacity of, say, less than a hundred, it is often worth supplying this information when seeking permission to perform; a reduced royalty payment may result. It is obviously to an author's advantage to earn *something* from his play rather than nothing at all because you cannot afford to produce it. If you are in any doubt as to whether royalties are payable at all, it is a fairly safe guide to assume that they are due at any time up to fifty years after the author's death, at which time they fall out of copyright. This is worth remembering, because you may be working from quite an old edition of a play which states that royalties are payable when in fact they no longer are. Please do be honest about royalties, though, and don't try to get away without paying them. The chances are that you might succeed, but it is grossly unfair to the author, without whose work you could not perform at all.

It is also helpful if the secretary can be responsible for ordering and obtaining a set of copies of the play, whether they are to be bought, borrowed from the local library, or hired from one of the organisations that have their own libraries. Remember that in addition to a copy each for members of the cast, you will also need them for the producer, stage-manager, lighting and sound effects technicians.

Printing of tickets, programmes and posters should also be dealt with early on as there is likely to be a matter of weeks between order and delivery. I have often found the printers of local newspapers best to undertake these jobs speedily, efficiently and at reasonable rates, but it might be worth looking around for a small, private part-time printer. Tickets can be very simple, but should be clearly marked with place, date and time of performance. If there are only to be two or three performances, I have often found it useful to have a different colour for each day as this helps avoid the embarrassment of double-booking.

If the producer is doing his job properly, he will have worked out at the beginning a full rehearsal schedule, with details of just what is to be covered and who will be involved at each session. This information is often conveyed by word of mouth, but that can lead to confusion and it is much more satisfactory if the secretary supplies each member of the cast with a typed copy of these instructions. It will, though, be a miracle if this schedule is adhered to implicitly, so amendments should also be notified in writing as soon as possible.

Should the production in hand be a costume piece, with all or some of the costumes to be hired, it will be necessary to obtain application forms from the costumiers. These will then have to be filled in for each member of the cast, in conjunction with the wardrobe mistress, and returned in good time. On arrival, the costumes should be checked against the order and, after the final performance, carefully re-checked before return.

Finally, the secretary might well be responsible for the control of petty cash. I have mentioned elsewhere the fact that a budget should have been established for every production, but this should include a small amount for items which have not been planned or foreseen. You will almost certainly find that the scene-builders suddenly run out of nails, screws or paint, or they need a small quantity of timber to complete the set. The lighting technician may discover that he doesn't, after all, have a sheet of gelatine that he needs, or perhaps the stage-manager will accidentally scratch a stylus across an all important record. These sort of things have to be paid for on the spot and a careful account of them kept so that production costs can be detailed accurately.

As performance date approaches it will be necessary for someone to organise and run the box-office. Small club theatres often manage to do this on a professional scale, with a box-office manned daily at regular hours, but the average dramatic society has to approach the job from a different angle. Members of the cast will probably sell tickets to families and friends in a rather haphazard sort of way, but it is essential to have someone in overall control. First, a seating plan should be drawn for each performance and, as tickets are sold, they must be marked off on these plans. It is also a good idea to keep a separate list of the names of all those who purchase tickets, with a cross-reference to the seating plan as a double check. It is best to be quite firm, too, in insisting that tickets are only handed over in return for cash. If they are distributed on promises only, you will find it leads to confusion, unsold returns at the last moment, and two lots of patrons arriving for the same seats. In conclusion, it is always worth reserving a few house seats for each performance to be issued as complimentaries, to the press, visiting dignitaries, or friends of the management!

I deliberately gave this chapter the somewhat grandiose title of Front of House Management, because this is the department in which so many dramatic societies are badly let down. I have seen many a good performance on stage spoiled by inefficiency in the auditorium, when this could so easily have been avoided by a little care and planning. The main duty of the front of house manager is to look after the comfort of the customers, and he must supervise programme sellers, ticket collectors and ushers, and bar and refreshment staff. But more important, perhaps, he is also the final tenuous link between back-stage and audience – the one bearer of physical communication between the two.

The FOH manager should arrive at the theatre quite early on performance evenings, in fact at about the same time as the stage-manager, and it is not a bad idea for the two to make contact with each other straight away, as they are going to be in touch from time to time for the rest of the evening. He should then distribute a float of small change to the box-office, if tickets still remain to be sold, to programme sellers and to refreshment staff, keeping a careful record of how much he has handed over in each case. He should also know exactly how many programmes each seller has to start with. In his initial liaison with the stage-manager he should have agreed a cueing system between the two of them, so that they can exchange the information that the audience is in and the curtain is ready to go up. In a permanent theatre with sophisticated equipment this will probably be by means of lights, buzzers or intercom, but in most cases will probably involve a quick personal visit. Before that most of his time until the commencement of the performance can be spent in the capacity of host, welcoming patrons personally. He will be informed by one of the means mentioned above when the stage-manager has called beginners and should then use any means he can to persuade the audience to take their seats, especially if they are showing a tendency to linger in the bar! Once they are in, it is his turn to return a cue to the SM so that he can start. Now, if the lighting system includes control of the houselights, these will be faded by the electrician, but if, as is so often the case, they are controlled by separate switches in the auditorium, the FOH manager must see that all lights are out before cueing the SM. All too often a curtain is taken up with half the house lights still on and this is terribly unsettling for an audience as well as distracting for the cast.

During the performance, the manager must check the take of his programme sellers, deduct the float he gave them in the first place, and then make sure that the difference equates with the number of programmes sold. He should also check the ticket stubs in his possession with the booking plan, and helpers on the door will have informed him of any seats remaining empty so that he can direct late arrivals to them with the minimum of disturbance to everyone else. Incidentally, I have often been tempted to follow the lead of some professional theatres in refusing admission after curtain up until the interval, though I've never had the heart – or perhaps the courage – to carry it out.

The times of intervals should have been calculated fairly accurately in advance, though these may vary slightly as a result of a late start or even of excessive laughter from the audience. However, the SM should give a warning cue about five minutes before each interval so that bar or refreshment staff can be alerted, drinks poured in readiness, or coffee and sandwiches put out. There is almost invariably a scramble for service in fairly restricted surroundings, so the more that can be prepared in advance the better. By the way, I do think that every effort should be made to supply either coffee or soft drinks at the very least. One society I visit regularly never bothers to do this and some of their patrons understandably feel constrained to nip over the green to the village local at the first interval. Unfortunately, they don't always come back!

As a final touch, may I suggest that you always try to provide either a wooden clock-face, or even a blackboard, somewhere near the main entrance carrying the information 'This performance ends at . . .' This knowledge is often useful to customers who have trains or buses to catch and may possibly prevent some of them from creeping out during the last few minutes. It is perhaps regrettable, but nevertheless true, that all members of an audience will not necessarily share the enthusiasm of the cast. In some cases they may have been press-ganged into attending at all. A smoothly efficient FOH manager can do much to make them feel both welcome and comfortable, and may even convert the reluctant into becoming regular play-goers.

Chapter 14

Final Thoughts

A misnomer for a chapter if ever there was one, for every time I think I have covered all the ground for putting on a play I remember something else I should add. Perhaps one of the most fascinating aspects of taking up amateur dramatics as a hobby is that no one ever really learns all that that there is to know. Any keenly dedicated actor or producer may feel that he is getting better as the years go by, but he will always see room for improvement in his efforts. As technical ability increases so will the desire to give freer rein to imagination in the endless quest for even better results. However, this book has to end somewhere, so I have read carefully through everything written so far and made a few notes on one or two items missed out.

For example, I find that I have said nothing at all about prompting. Now all too often this important aspect of performance is left until the last minute, when a possibly reluctant back-stage helper is pressed into the work with little or no preparation. This can be worse than having no prompt at all, for good prompting is almost an art in itself.

I recommend finding someone who is willing to undertake this job as early as possible during rehearsals and a good source is often the cast members' relatives, or friends with no desire to perform themselves. They are often keen to help and find this preferable to being left alone during the long period of rehearsals.

The first thing a prompter must do is pay careful attention to the producer's instructions concerning pauses and mark these in the text. He will then learn, together with the actors during rehearsal, how to 'feel' those pauses. This is essential, for there are few things more irritating to a performer than getting a prompt when it is not needed. There is a story, probably apochryphal, about the old actor Macready who was said to have as part of his stock-in-trade three degrees of pause: ordinary, long and grand. During a performance at which the regular prompter had been replaced temporarily there came a moment of silence which seemed to the newcomer to go on far too long, so he nervously supplied the next line. A wounded Macready boomed sadly back, 'Laddie, you've prompted me during me Grand Pause!'

It is useful if the prompter is as well acquainted with the whole text as members of the cast, for ideally he should be able to keep one eye on the stage and the other on the book. It is often easier, to *see* rather than to *hear* when a prompt is needed. Furthermore, he is almost certain to find that occasions arise when the cast will inadvertently cut lines or even whole speeches, but if what is heard is familiar he should be able to find the place fairly quickly. In fairness, I should admit that I have sometimes been guilty of this and then, realising that what I had cut was essential to the plot, have gone back again and put it in. I don't suppose I am the only actor to have done so, but this can be fairly hair-raising for the prompt corner. There is another story to illustrate this point about a cast getting themselves into a hopeless muddle and finally drying completely. One actor sidled towards the wings and hissed, 'What's the line?' Meeting with no response, he edged even closer to the corner and said, 'What's the bloody line?' This time the flustered prompter, thumbing desperately through the text, replied heatedly, 'What's the bloody line? What's the bloody *play?*'

The other important factor to bear in mind is exactly *how* to give a prompt. To my mind there is only one way, and that is firmly, clearly and audibly. There is no doubt that when the need for a prompt arises it is an embarrassing moment for both actors and audience, but it is fatal to give the prompt in a whisper in the hope that the audience will not hear it. The chances are that the actor will not hear it either, thereby prolonging the agony. For this reason I always prefer to have a girl on the book, because a lighter feminine voice tends to be more audible, despite being perhaps masked by a flat or a curtain.

In a conventional proscenium-arch theatre, the prompter is traditionally situated in the corner down left, which has occasioned that side of the stage being called the prompt side, and the other, obviously, the opposite prompt (or OP) side. With an open stage or theatre in the round, clearly a different situation will have to be found, but it is the ideal in any circumstances for the prompter at all times to have a clear view of the whole stage. This may not always be possible, indeed in my own theatre it is quite *im*possible, and this underlines the necessity for the prompter to be thoroughly acquainted with the play and the production.

To summarise, then, the prompter should attend all rehearsals from the time the producer orders books to be put down by actors, for she will be able to help them immeasurably with learning their lines and will also get to know them herself. When a prompt becomes necessary in performance she must give it loud and clear, and at all times she must give one hundred per cent concentration.

There is one more story about prompting, and this time a true one, told me by Marius Goring. Many years ago, as a young actor, he was appearing with Robert Atkins' company in the open-air season in Regent's Park. One of the plays in the repertoire was *A Midsummer Night's Dream* in which Atkins himself played the part of Peter Quince, leader and producer of the Rude Mechanicals. In the scene where they gather in the woods to rehearse their play of 'Pyramus and Thisbe' he had added a bit of business which required the cast to skip around the stage in a rustic dance until they all gathered down centre. On one occasion they had completed the first lap, when Atkins noticed that one character was missing, so he hissed to the others, 'Go round again.' This happened a second and a third time, when the poor prompter thought he must have dried and so threw him the line, 'Are we all met?' This added insult to injury for Robert Atkins, who stalked towards the prompter and said in his famous stage whisper. 'Of course we're not all – met. Do you think we'd be doing this bloody silly dance if we were?'

In the course of those few thoughts on prompting I mentioned that we refer to the left and right sides of the stage as the Prompt and Opposite Prompt respectively. The P and OP abbreviations are also commonly used for marking pieces of scenery to facilitate their assembly on stage. For example, if you have had to make a box set away from the theatre, it is useful to number all the pieces on the back. Starting from the down left corner, each flat should be clearly marked P1. P2, P3, etc., round to up-stage centre. Then starting from down right mark them OP 1, OP 2, and so on.

The matter of storing scenery will probably present many societies with their biggest problem. As different situations all give rise to their own particular headaches there is no textbook answer to them. I can only tell you how we have dealt with them ourselves. The first society for whom I produced put on plays in the local village hall four times a year. We were only able to book the hall for a week on each occasion, so that the first Sunday had to be spent building, or at least assembling sets. We were allowed, however, to store flats underneath the stage since the space there was of little or no use to anyone else using the hall. It is perhaps worth mentioning that those flats had to be treated to make them fire-proof and we were visited quite regularly by a fire prevention officer to make sure we had complied with this regulation. Had we not done so, he was empowered to prevent the performance taking place. In many halls these requirements extend to your completed set and to everything on it, including curtains for example, so do make sure you know the rules at the theatre where you plan to present your plays. This may seem to an impatient producer just another piece of irritating bureaucracy, but I can only say that it is a wise precaution. The village hall I referred to was in fact a replacement for one burned down a week before a play was due to open, destroying an elaborate set, costumes and props which had *not* been treated.

Of course, even with a full set of flats ready made, one day is all too little to assemble a complete set. I used therefore to have other pieces made well in advance and stored away from the hall. One of our workers had a large barn workshop with plenty of space, and we found a local farmer who was prepared to rent us a trailer cheaply to transport items back and forth.

In my own small theatre at present, space is really at a premium, but at least I have the advantage that the stage is never used for any other purpose. When a production ends, therefore, I leave the set in place until it is time to start building the next. In addition, I have built a rack of metal strips suspended from the beams of my garage, and these hold all our spare timber. Then a near neighbour has at the bottom of his garden a large, disused, brick pig-sty, where he kindly allows me to store still further pieces of scenery that are too useful in the long term to be destroyed or dismantled. However, on that last point, I would urge all societies to be, certainly not wasteful, but quite ruthless in deciding what is worth keeping for future use. Quite often an item will represent hours of work and may have been tremendously effective in use, but before you decide to keep it do ask yourself seriously whether you are ever *likely* to want it again. Another group I worked with had a scenic director who was notorious for keeping every mortal thing that was used in every play. *He* claimed to know where everything was, but finding it often made the proverbial search for the needle in the haystack child's play by comparison.

Costume storage can also present difficulties, but two thoughts are perhaps worth registering. It is always better to hang clothes on a rack than to store them in a skip, for they are then instantly ready for use without being full of creases. Always see that they are cleaned after a production, and try to keep a catalogue of everything you have got. This could save you pounds in hire charges. By the way, if you are able to build up your own wardrobe, do make frequent checks against damage by moths.

A final word on the subject of storing items that you are going to need every time you do a play; don't forget the lighting department. We keep three large boxes: one contains a supply of spare bulbs and lamps (the spares being immediately replaced as items are taken into use), another houses various sizes of gelatine frames, and the third a good selection of sheets of gelatine. The main reason for this is that I have found in practice that these are the sort of things one invariably needs at a time when it is impossible to get out and buy new supplies. It seems to be a fact of life in spite of my frequent remarks about planning in advance.

Now I see from my notes that I promised in an earlier chapter to return to the subject of dialect speech. This is something that crops up in plays with great regularity and is often regarded as a frightening hurdle. Most amateur actors seem capable of producing a sort of cockney, a sort of north country, and an oddity known as 'mummerset' for all and any country characters. These generally bear little or no resemblance to true regional dialects and will be instantly spotted by an audience as phoney. When it comes to producing an acceptable American dialect, most professional English actors seem to flounder as well.

There are numerous prescribed ways of learning to play a role with an authentic dialect, but I have found only one that really works. I call it the 'soundtrack of the mind.' I find a voice with exactly the characteristics I wish to emulate, perhaps on record, radio or television, or produced by someone known to me personally, and then listen to it with utmost concentration at every opportunity. Eventually I find that this has resulted in a sort of 'sound memory' so that I can look at printed words and hear the voice of the chosen person saying those words in my mind's ear as clearly as if he were in the room with me. Then I attempt to speak the words aloud, using my own natural tone quality but employing all the other characteristics that I can hear on that mental soundtrack. I stress that point about using one's own natural tones, because therein lies the fundamental difference between learning a dialect and simply giving an impersonation of another known personality.

There is in the BBC gramophone library a remarkable set of records covering every known dialect in the British Isles, though I don't suppose this is available to the general public. You would certainly be unlikely to find anything like it in your friendly neighbourhood disc shop. But it might be worth enquiring at the record department of the local library whether they have anything on these lines. However, your radio and television provide you with a marvellous source of dialects, not necessarily in plays, but in documentaries and news programmes. If you are lucky enough to anticipate the right programme, try to record it. The actual words being spoken are relatively unimportant, for it is the *characteristics* of speech that you need. Play your recording over and over to yourself, until you think you can reproduce the dialect yourself, and then turn your attention to the lines in your play and try to hear that voice reading them. It may come easily to some, and not to others, but I feel sure that with concentration and practice you will find that it works for you.

I have made several references in the course of this book to the performance of Shakespeare by amateur societies, but there are still a few points I think worthy of mention. It seems to me, after many years of observation, that many groups regard the works of our greatest national playwright as sacrosanct, with every word and every character inviolate. That is an attitude perhaps more appropriate to the classroom than to the stage, and let us not lose sight of the fact that, however little we know about Shakespeare the man, there is no doubt that he was not only a dramatist but a man of the theatre. He acted himself, wrote parts for particular members of his own company and, I am sure, changed lines and scenes to order. A genius he was, but a practical man to boot. I firmly believe that he would approve a firm editorial approach to make his works acceptable to a twentieth-century audience. For example, there are very few so-called 'clown scenes' in his plays which convey much to us today. Jokes which set Elizabethan audiences in a roar fall, if not on deaf, at least on dumbfounded contemporary ears. Be ruthless, and prune them freely.

Again, it may surprise you to find how many characters you can lose without seriously diminishing the dramatic validity of the play. To cite a rather drastic example, I once took a production of *Hamlet* on a tour of schools. After long deliberation we decided to cut out all the Rosencrantz and Guildenstern scenes; we left Fortinbras off stage, and we reduced the two grave-diggers to one. This pruning down to the main and chief subsidiary plots was much praised by pupils and teaching staff at the schools we visited. This approach cuts the running time to something in the region of two and a half hours, and needless to say is a great help to societies with the perennial problem of man shortage.

I must also mention the invaluable ploy of doubling certain roles to save on man-power. As a matter of fact I feel utterly convinced that Shakespeare wrote often with this specific purpose in mind, since so many of his plays feature characters early on who vanish at the half-way point, while new characters are often introduced in the fourth or fifth act. Even professional companies have taken advantage of this factor since time immemorial. Let me quote just a few examples. I was once a member of an Old Vic company, playing *Henry V*, in which Paul Rogers very successfully doubled the Dauphin with the Duke of Burgundy. It was a *tour de force* for him, and in a way an added attraction for the audience. Again, in a recent production of *As You Like It* I found that I was able to ask one actor to double the courtier, Le Beau, in early scenes, with that of the yokel William, who appears later on. Another player provided the old shepherd in the middle of the play, and Orlando's young brother in the final scene. Doubling can have other advantages, for it is often possible to create one worthwhile part out of several small ones. Shakespeare often uses 'A Lord' or 'A Servant' at random to help provide dialogue with principal characters, and these can often be played by one actor, building his part up into a real and distinct personality.

And as a final word on Shakespeare, may I suggest that you keep your sets to a minimum? By all means dress the play attractively, but let the poetry stir your audience's imagination as it was intended to originally. Shakespeare knew what he was at when he gave his *Henry V* chorus the words:

'. . . can this cockpit hold
The vasty fields of France? or may we cram
Within this wooden O the very casques
That did affright the air at Agincourt?'

The answer to that question can be a resounding 'Yes!'

And there we are. With these words, drawings and photographs I have tried to show you not how *you* should go about putting on a play, but how I have done it these many years. At least, how I have tried to do it. Obviously I have had to compromise in all areas of presenting plays, but I still maintain, as I said at the beginning, that it is always best to start out pursuing the ideal. The theatre has provided me with a way of life that is colourful and exciting at times, but always absorbing. As a hobby it can do the same for you, and I hope it will.